Theology and Practice

Theology and Practice

Edited by Duncan B. Forrester

EPWORTH PRESS

© Epworth Press 1990

British Library Cataloguing in Publication Data

Forrester, Duncan B
Theology and practice.
1. Theology
I. Title
230

ISBN 0–7162–0466–5

First published 1990
by Epworth Press
Room 195, 1 Central Buildings,
Westminster, London SW1H 9NR

Phototypeset by J&L Composition Ltd, Filey, N. Yorkshire
and printed in Great Britain by
Billing & Sons Ltd, Worcester

Contents

Preface

This is a book of essays by recent and present members of the teaching staff of the Department of Christian Ethics and Practical Theology in the University of Edinburgh. For upward of ten years we have enjoyed one another's company. We have stimulated and sometimes provoked one another by discussing and arguing about the kind of issues with which these chapters engage, by commenting on one another's work, and by the simple fact that we have derived immense satisfaction from the work we have been privileged to undertake together. Our students have constantly kept us on our toes and have shared fully and energetically in a common enterprise. Four of the contributors have now left the Department; Alastair Campbell to a chair in New Zealand, Robin Gill to a research professorship in Newcastle, David Lyall to St Andrews University, and Murray Leishman to the Scottish Institute of Human Relations. We miss them, and are grateful for all they have given to our Department. And, as the Department welcomes what is today known in the academic world as 'new blood', we hope that the future will be as lively and productive as the past.

The connecting thread of the various chapters, and the central concern of the Department, is the relation of theory and practice, an issue which must today bulk large in the responsible doing of theology. If a theory independently established is expected to shape and determine practice, or practice is seen as simply deduced from theory, or as the application of theory, theology as such would become pure theory, distanced from practice. For various reasons Christian theology has difficulty in accommodating itself to this model. Indeed today numerous theologians are proclaiming the priority of praxis (e.g. J.-B. Metz), or stating that 'the new criterion of theology and of faith is to be found in praxis' (Moltmann). The original stimulus for much of this kind of thought is to be found in Marxism. It was Marx himself who wrote in the *Theses on Feuerbach* (1845): 'The question of whether objective truth can be attributed to human thinking is not a question of theory, but a practical question. In practice man must prove the truth, that is the reality and power, the this-sidedness of his thinking... The philosophers have only interpreted the world, in various ways; the point, however, is to change it.'

But sometimes theologians who find in such sentiments useful reminders of the nature of Christian truth assert the primacy of praxis in a rather simplistic way, as if understanding of theory emerged spontaneously and effortlessly out of immersion in activity. In fact a productive dialectical relationship between theory and practice of the sort Marx was advocating is far from easy to establish or sustain; but it is essential if theology is indeed to be an authentically Christian practical science. Theory and practice belong together; separation distorts each. Too much theology, like the philosophy Marx attacks, has been an interpretation, and by implication a justification, of the world. But theology surely has to do with practice, with changing the world, with conversion, with the mission of the church, and with the attempt to understand reality and live life within the perspective of the Kingdom. The practice of the church thus strives to anticipate the practice of the Kingdom, and the church's proclamation of this Kingdom to all humankind reminds us that the church is concerned not with narrow matters of institutional survival or enlargement, but with the nature and destiny of the human family and the cosmos, with 'God's plan for the fullness of time, to unite all things in Christ, things in heaven and things on earth' (Eph. 1.10).

The studies in this book represent some of our particular concerns within the overarching commitment to explore the relation of theory and practice in theology. They range from discussions of the nature of the subject, through the place of the Bible in practical theology, to the examination of theory and practice in specific areas of ministry. They are offered in the hope that they will help to stimulate further discussion and study in these important areas. The authors are indebted to one another, to colleagues in the hospitals, in various ministries, and in other departments in the University, as well as to our students, for stimulus and criticism. Chapters one and two represent revised versions of articles which appeared in the *Scottish Journal of Theology* 33 (1979) and 25 (1972). We are grateful to the publishers for permission to use this material here. The Revd David Sinclair, one of our research students, assisted with the proofs and compiled the index, while Mrs Elspeth Leishman and Mrs Sheena Carlyle dealt with the preparation of the type script with tireless efficiency. We are grateful to them.

New College, Edinburgh   Duncan B. Forrester
February 1990

Contributors

Alastair V. Campbell was until recently Senior Lecturer and Head of the Department of Christian Ethics and Practical Theology in Edinburgh University. Among his books are *Rediscovering Pastoral Care* (1981, [2]1986), *Moral Dilemmas in Medicine* (1972, [3]1984), *Moderated Love: A Theology of Professional Care* (1984) and *The Gospel of Anger* (1986). In 1989 he took up a Personal Chair in Biomedical Ethics in the Medical Faculty of the University of Otago, New Zealand.

Duncan B. Forrester has been Professor of Christian Ethics and Practical Theology since 1978, and Principal of New College since 1986. His publications include *Caste and Christianity* (1980), *Encounter with God* (with J. I. H. McDonald and Gian Tellini, 1983), *Christianity and the Future of Welfare* (1985), *Theology and Politics* (1988) and *Beliefs, Values and Policies: Conviction Politics in a Secular Age* (1989).

Robin Gill was Senior Lecturer in the Edinburgh Department of Christian Ethics and Practical Theology and has been since January 1989 William Leech Research Professor in Applied Christian Theology in the University of Newcastle upon Tyne. Among the books that he has had published are: *Theology and Social Structure* (1977), *A Textbook of Christian Ethics* (1985), *Theology and Sociology: A Reader* (1987), *Beyond Decline* (1988) and *Competing Convictions* (1989).

Murray Leishman was for many years Chaplain to the Royal Edinburgh Hospital, a major psychiatric teaching hospital, and part-time Lecturer in Pastoral Theology. He is now a psychotherapist on the staff of the Scottish Institute of Human Relations.

David Lyall was Chaplain to the Edinburgh Northern Group of Hospitals and part-time Lecturer in Pastoral Theology. Since 1987 he has been Lecturer in Practical Theology in St Mary's College, University of St Andrews. He is Editor of *Contact – The Interdisciplinary Journal of Pastoral Studies* and has published (with John Foskett) *Helping the Helpers: Supervision and Pastoral Care* (1988).

J. Ian H. McDonald is Lecturer in Christian Ethics and in New Testament. His publications include *Kerygma and Didache* (1980), *Encounter with God* (1983, with Duncan Forrester and Gian Tellini), *The Quest for Christian Ethics* (1984, with Ian Fairweather), *Jesus and the Ethics of the Gospel* (1987, with Bruce Chilton), and *The Resurrection: Narrative and Belief* (1989). He is currently at work on a study of the nature of New Testament ethics.

I

A Practical Theology for Today?

1

Divinity in Use and Practice

Duncan B. Forrester

'Divinity', said Martin Luther, 'consists in use and practice, not in speculation and meditation. Everyone that deals in speculations, either in household affairs or temporal government, without practice, is lost and worth nothing.'[1] And elsewhere, more strongly: 'true theology is practical ... speculative theology belongs with the devil in hell.'[2] But *can* theology be *practical*? The conventional stereotype of theology in the modern world is as the most impractical of all disciplines, the very epitome of irrelevance. The friendly banter we sometimes receive from secular colleagues who regard the title 'practical theology' as a contradiction in terms demands some kind of apologia which goes beyond a nervous reminder that there are still religious professionals who require training for the fulfilment of their duties. After all, we claim that theology has a relevance and a significance far beyond the shaping of ministerial activity.

It is not just the intellectual credentials of the particular discipline of practical theology, but the right of theology to a place in the academy, and indeed the proper bearing of matters of theory and principle on the life of action which are at issue. The former British Prime Minister, Harold Wilson, was voicing the pragmatic prejudices of his generation when he denounced with derision attempts to discuss political principles as just 'theology' – in other words, an unproductive luxury which is a distraction from the serious business of seeking efficiency, success, economic growth and all the unexamined and often conflicting values of the 1960s and 1970s.

In more recent days in Britain and elsewhere an even more alarming edge has been added to the popular use of the term 'theology', as doctrinaire adherence to economic theories which seem capable of no form of confirmation or refutation, and in application have the most grievous social consequences, is described as a 'theological stance'. With the arrival of the New Right we have entered a new era, the age of 'conviction politics'. No one any longer proclaims 'the death of ideology' (Daniel Bell); it is clearly alive and well. But in 'conviction politics' policies are not based on open discussion and the attempt to achieve some general agreement about the goals of society, or on careful attention to the facts of the case. Indeed since 1979 there has been a dramatic reduction in governmental collection of data and neither Royal Commissions nor prolonged and open periods of consultation precede the enactment of legislation effecting fundamental changes in society. Neither empirical evidence nor informed but contrary opinions are allowed to challenge conclusions which spring from invulnerable dogmas about human beings, and society, and the way things are and how they ought to be.

When efforts are made to root these dogmas in the Christian gospel, as was done very explicitly in Mrs Thatcher's speech to the General Assembly of the Church of Scotland in 1988, not only is a dangerously oversimplified view of the relation of beliefs and policies presented, but the very integrity of the gospel is at stake.[3] Critical and responsible theology must ask whether it is a true or a false gospel which is being proclaimed and protest against the ideological use of theology. There is a crisis and a challenge to theology when the gospel is reduced to slogans or weapons which the prosperous and powerful use to defend their privilege against the weak and poor.

The issue is essentially one of truth. It was Pilate, sitting in judgment upon Jesus who, according to John's Gospel, asked the question, 'What is truth?' only to brush it aside in order to proceed to actions which could not but have been deeply affected had he pursued his question until it received an answer. To have continued the discussion, he may have felt, would have been a political luxury which might have led him into a morass of profitless verbal polemics; certainly it would inhibit him from the immediate and decisive action for which the people were clamouring and to which expediency counselled him. As only too commonly, the refusal to take the question of truth with ultimate seriousness leads to practice which is ill-considered and dangerously responsive to the pressures of the powerful and of the moment. And so we may start with the suggestion that practical theology is *that branch of theology which is concerned with questions of truth in relation to action.* This points to a deep reciprocity between theory and practice, whereby theological understanding not only leads to action, but also arises out of practice, involvement in the life of the world: 'He who does what is true comes to the light' (John 3.21). Practical theology is therefore concerned with the doing of the truth, and with the encounter with truth in action, with what the French philosopher Roger Garaudy calls 'the active nature of knowledge'.[4]

Much of our thinking in this area has been dominated, not entirely helpfully, by the Greek duality between the *vita activa* and the *vita contemplativa*, and by the corresponding distinction between the practical and theoretical sciences. The Greek understanding of the nature of the two life-styles and the relation between them was not uniform. Plato exalted the contemplative life so far above the life of action that his Guardians, who had been illumined by a training in contemplation, had to be induced unwillingly to engage in the only kind of practice which possessed real significance, that is, ruling. Their task was to bring down from heaven, as it were, a blue-print of the ideal state and soul, and impose this on an infinitely malleable society and its individual citizens. The Guardians' wisdom did not arise out of their experience of ruling, but was brought to it from their comprehension of the Form of the Good. Practice must conform to theory; it is not itself in any way constitutive of truth. And as for the practice of the lower orders, indeed almost all practice apart from ruling, these were of little interest and related to nothing that could be dignified as wisdom or science. Aristotle, on the other hand, emphasized something which he called *phronesis*, or practical wisdom, which relates directly to action. Yet despite his more positive view of practice, when pressed Aristotle, hardly less than Plato, asserts the superiority of the *vita contemplativa* over the *vita activa*, of *theoria* over *praxis*.

Closely related to this duality, indeed in many ways an alternative formulation of it, is another which may be indicated by the contrast between Dionysus and Apollo. Dionysus represents the affective life, the emotions and the passions – joy, fear, pain, delight, love, anger, and so on. Dionysus stands for the feelings as a central part of what it means to be human. Apollo, on the other hand, stands for reason, for the claim of the head to rule over the heart. The main philosophic tradition was strongly Apollonian, and looked askance at all that Dionysus signified. Emotions might need some outlet, even among educated and enlightened people, hence the festivals of sexuality in Plato's *Republic*. But emotions are seen as dangerous, unpredictable, subhuman, irrational; they must be controlled if they are not to be disruptive of social order, of rationality, of wisdom. Hence Socrates dies without fear or regret, secure in the knowledge that such events do not matter, and that it is unseemly for a philosopher to be emotional. And by way of Stoicism a heavy emphasis on the need to control, to curb, to master the emotions has penetrated deep into the Christian tradition. The reference to Apollo and Dionysus reminds us that this duality reflects two contrary ideas of God: the god of the philosophers is apathetic, impassible, detached, uninvolved and the philosopher should model himself on him. Dionysus is pure emotion, uncontrolled, unpredictable, spontaneous, shown best in ecstasy or orgy. His followers imitate him, taking as their slogan David Hume's reversal of the Stoics' wisdom: 'Reason is, and ought to be, the slave of the passions.'

The Christian theologian nurtures a distinctive unease with this kind of dualistic thought. He cannot accept the philosophers' depreciation of action which runs so deep, nor the suspicion of emotion. On the other hand, the theologian does not reverse the classical priorities; rather he must transcend the duality. For he knows that understanding and doing, theory and practice, contemplation and action, reason and emotion – and especially loving and knowing – are integrally related and interdependent. Above all, perhaps, he is mindful that the wisdom of God become incarnate in a man, who wrought our salvation through his active and passive obedience to the Father. The Logos – that term for the rational principle of the universe beloved of the Stoics – acts. He goes, like Dionysus, to a wedding party. His prayers and his teaching, his deeds and his suffering make a strange unity such that one cannot allocate him either to the active or to the contemplative role. He belongs to both, or to neither, for he draws the two into a harmony.

It is not simply that theology accords to practice a greater significance than did the Greeks; it has a far broader and more complex notion of the nature of practice. The practice with which the theologian is concerned ranges from the world-transforming political praxis which figures so largely in the important and challenging work of the liberation theologians to the practical faithfulness and love of the simple believer in work and relationships; and it must encompass passion in both its senses, as suffering and, more generally, as emotion.

Luther suggests that the *via crucis* is a third way, and the specifically Christian way, which embraces and transcends both the *vita contemplativa* and the *vita activa*: 'We must beware,' he writes, 'that the active life with its work and the contemplative life with its speculations do not lead us astray. Both are very attractive and peaceful, but for that reason also dangerous, until they are tempered by the cross and disturbed by adversaries. But the cross is the safest of all.'[5]

Furthermore, if theology is compelled to choose between regarding itself as a 'pure' theoretical science in the Greek sense or a practical science (and it would do well to resist the terms in which the choice is posed), it cannot but opt for the latter. For theology is not a detached, dispassionate endeavour to understand the things of God, but the coming to know God in striving to do his will: it 'consists in use and practice'. An immediate implication of this, of course, is that theology, and particularly Practical Theology, must pursue its task in the closest dialogue with the other practical social sciences, open to their insights and ready to contribute its own. To mention but one instance of the profitability of such an enterprise from modern times: it is hardly possible to exaggerate the contribution of Reinhold Niebuhr, operating strictly as a theologian, to the secular study of politics and international relations.

Much of what has been said so far relates to theology as a whole; but within theology there has perforce to be a division of labour, although not such that the various theological disciplines neglect dialogue with each other or refuse to cultivate the fascinating borderlands between specific branches of theology, and between theological and secular studies. The peculiar responsibilities of Practical Theology involve acting as a bridge between theology and the social sciences and reflecting critically upon, learning from, and endeavouring to renew, reform and strengthen practice and, in particular, Christian practice.

Practical Theology is not 'applied theology', if that term implies that the practical theologian receives ready-made the results fed in by the biblical and systematic theologians and considers, as the practical theologian's part, how these conclusions may be put to work. If this rather platonic account were accurate, the subject would merit the title sometimes given it in Scotland in the past by irreverent students by the addition of two letters: 'practically theology': ancillary to the other subjects, but hardly a theological discipline in its own right. In dealing with communication – and specifically with homiletics – for example, the practical theologian is concerned, as are all theologians, with the content of the message no less than with the techniques of putting it across. As a theologian, not a sophist or public relations specialist, teaching students how to make friends and influence people, the practical theologian's distinctive contribution arises from a special concern with the contemporary context, relevance, and relation to practice of the message preached.

Wolfhart Pannenberg has pointed out that 'any fundamental consideration of the meaning and function of practical theology must clarify the concept of practice which gives it its name'.[6] It is not enough, I would suggest, to confine the practice with which the practical theologian is concerned with the traditional subdivisions of homiletics, liturgics, catechetics, pastoralia and ethics. We need a broader understanding of practice within which the traditional subdivisions may be studied in their proper perspective. We are also reminded forcefully by the political theologians of the Third World that Christian practice is not adequately regarded as either the fulfilment by clergy of a traditional, accepted role within an unquestioned ecclesiastical structure, or churchly activity which reflects and legitimates the established order of things. Rather, they say, it has at its centre world-transforming political activity. This should be received as a friendly corrective to much of our timidity and narrowness. The fact that so many Christians in various lands have come to see the path of obedience to Christ as necessarily involving political commitment to radical change, and a positive identification with the oppressed and exploited, must come as a challenge to our sometimes very conventional and parochial undertakings of Christian practice and of theology.

Within such a context practical theologians concern themselves with what in other traditions is labelled 'priestly formation', and in the churches of the Reformation, the practical training of the ministry, but we cannot do this without looking to the priestly formation of the whole *laos*, the equipping of all the saints for the work of ministry. Furthermore, our concern is with reformation rather than formation, for increasingly the call of God is to do the unprecedented, and traditional forms of Christian practice are subjected these days to a questioning which is a fundamental challenge to renewal. Within such a context we strive to prepare a ministry committed to the Lord, sensitive to the needs of the age, and imbued with a vision of the church which is ecumenical and world-wide. Practical Theology today cannot, and must not, provide an induction into a fully recognized, secure and sheltered pattern of ministerial practice. This is partly because there is in church and society so much exhilarating and liberating uncertainty about the role of the minister, but more significantly because ministerial practice is *semper reformandum* and must be constantly scrutinized in the light of new theological insights, and deeper knowledge of contemporary society.

I have said enough to make it clear that Practical Theology is, in my opinion, a churchly discipline. But this does not imply that it accepts without question the validity of the existing practice of the churches. It is involved rather in a dialectical inter-action between the practice of the churches and theology, which must both be understood within the horizon of the Kingdom into which men and women of every tribe and tongue and people and nation are at the last to be gathered.[7] That is why missiology is so important in Practical Theology, and why all fruitful Practical Theology must today be profoundly ecumenical. Practical Theology strives to engage with questions of truth in relation to practice in general, to Christian practice, and to ministerial practice. It bases its work on the conviction that there is a unity of theory and practice. And the final object of its enquiries is nothing less than the equipment of pilgrims for the use and practice of their true home land.

2

The Nature of Practical Theology

Alastair V. Campbell

Some academic subject matters have a quaintly old fashioned ring; 'moral sciences' for example or 'natural philosophy'. 'Practical theology' has a similar odd sound today. To the theological outsider it must sound remarkably like a contradiction in terms, whilst to the professional theologian it may carry undertones of an unscholarly pragmatism or a tendency towards liberal theology. Yet perhaps the juxtaposition of these two terms is an important one. It may, by its oddity, encourage us to ask the question, 'Is practical theology possible?' This would be a question similar to the familiar one about the possibility of metaphysics. It is asking for a formal definition of the subject matter which will meet adequate criteria of meaning, consistency and relationship to other disciplines whose status is not in doubt. In this chapter I shall attempt some answers to this question of possibility, by focussing specifically on writings in the theology of pastoral care.

Although it may sound antiquarian, the term 'practical theology' appears to be of relatively recent usage. It first makes its appearance in German nineteenth-century theological treatises, the most celebrated of which was F. D. E. Schleiermacher's posthumous work, *Die Praktische Theologie nach den Grundsätzen der Evangelischen Kirche*.[1] Schleiermacher described it as the 'crown of theological studies', its tasks being the setting out of 'the method of the maintaining (*Erhaltung*) and perfecting (*Vervollkommnung*) of the church'.[2] This emphasis on the church-based nature of the discipline is an important one for the subsequent development of practical theology, particularly when we remember that in Schleiermacher's terms the church is the fellowship of those who share in God-consciousness.

In other nineteenth-century text books, the subject was sub-divided into various branches related to the different functions of the ministry: homiletics, liturgics, catechetics, poimenics and occasionally halieutics ('man fishing') and works of charity. J. J. Van Oosterzee's large volume[3] provides a good illustration of this approach. It contains a wealth of common-sense advice to trainee ministers concerning preaching, conduct of services, catechetical instruction, and both 'general' and 'individual' pastoral care. Significantly, a very short concluding section mentions 'labours beyond the sphere of one's own congregation'. The author feels uncertain whether such non-congregational matters are strictly within the domain of practical theology.

As the text books multiplied in the late nineteenth century the concern with the teaching of techniques became paramount. Thus, as Seward Hiltner remarks in a brief historical sketch of the recent history of the subject:

> The notion of 'hints and helps', implying the right to dispense with structural and theoretical considerations, to set aside scholarship in this area, and to appeal to the more degraded forms of practicalism, helped to drive most systematic books out of this field by the turn of the century.[4]

Such a development meant that the discipline became divorced from the important new movements in systematic theology and biblical studies. Far from being the 'crown' of divinity it became its poor relation. We may note certain difficulties inherent in the basic approach to the subject which led to this collapse:

1. The relationship between practical theology and historical and dogmatic theology was seen largely as a deductive one, practical theology being understood as *applied* theology, just as, say, civil engineering is applied physics. Thus Oosterzee, arguing in the same terms as Schleiermacher that the other theological sciences exist to serve practical theology, declares that 'It teaches the minister of the Gospel to apply ... the knowledge which he has already acquired in the theoretic domain.'[5] Such a relationship, however, is not satisfactory for either side. On the one hand it removes the independent status

of practical theology, making it into a subsection of dogmatics, whilst on the other hand it opens systematic theologians to charges of irrelevance and inapplicability from practical theologians. The result of this uneasy relationship was the drifting apart of the two disciplines.

2. The question of whether practical theology was an 'art' or a 'science' remained unresolved. Where the subject became the teaching of techniques by 'craftsmen pastors' to 'apprentice pastors' it tended to degenerate into 'a pastoral medicine chest for all conceivable and inconceivable ailments',[6] and its status within an academic environment became questionable.

3. Most unfortunate of all was the total identification of the discipline with church-directed functions of ministry. Since the church was seen in Schleiermacher's terms as the fellowship of the pious, this meant the imprisoning of practical theology in the world of the religiously minded. One sees this most clearly in the dubious position which 'missions' and 'works of charity' had in the nineteenth-century view of the principal functions of ministry. Since the clergyman had become a kind of chaplain to the godly-minded, his relationship (and the relationship of the church he served) to the world outside became of secondary concern. Spiritual maintenance was the keynote and practical theology provided the manuals which well ensured the perfection of the church. This type of definition of the scope of the subject meant that it was quite ill-equipped to cope with the radical questioning of the place of the church in the world evident in post-liberal theology.

Can an approach to the subject be found which avoids these pitfalls? There appears to have been little interest in recent theological writing in the construction of a comprehensive definition of practical theology.[7] However, the area of the *theology of pastoral care* has received considerable attention and we may look to this field for the main lines of the contemporary debate.

From post war writing in the theology of pastoral care two works may be singled out for special attention: Eduard Thurneysen's *A Theology of Pastoral Care*, and Seward Hiltner's *Preface to Pastoral Theology*. Each book in its own way has attempted to set the theology of pastoral care within the general context of the subject matter of theology and each has implicitly a view of practical theology as a whole.

Thurneysen's definition is reminiscent in some respects of Schleiermacher's view. He states that '... pastoral care occurs within the realm of the church ... it presupposes membership in the body of Christ, or has this membership as its purpose'.[8] However, although Thurneysen's view of pastoral care is clearly church-centred, its ultimate definition derives from a theology of the Word of God. Pastoral care is concerned with the 'specific communication to the individual of the message proclaimed in general in the sermon to the congregation'.[9] The message to be proclaimed is that of the forgiveness which is at the heart of the Gospel.

One may see in this formulation of Thurneysen's one way of establishing coherence in the discipline of practical theology. The normative concept is that of the Word of God, which may take several forms in its communication to the believer. That aspect known as 'pastoral care' has as its *differentia* the uniqueness of the one-to-one encounter, but in the last analysis all is dependent on the Word as witnessed to in scripture and tradition. One could summarize Thurneysen's view by saying that practical theology is best understood on the homiletical model, the model of proclamation.

A very different view is put forward by Seward Hiltner in his *Preface to Pastoral Theology*. Hiltner proposes a division of the subject matter of divinity into two types of field: the 'logic-centred' field and the 'operation-centred' field. The first category includes within it biblical theology, historical theology and doctrinal theology. The second category is Hiltner's re-definition of practical theology. He subdivides the operation-centred field into three 'perspectives': Shepherding, Communicating and Organizing. These three perspectives replace the traditional division of practical theology into the offices of the ministry.

By using the term 'perspective' Hiltner is trying to convey the notion that there are several different ways of regarding the offices and functions of the church, each in itself a valid way. Anything that is done within the life of the church may be viewed from a shepherding (or pastoral) perspective, or from the perspective of communicating (compare Thurneysen's proclamation category) or that of organizing (that area traditionally described as church discipline). Against the background of this restructuring of the subject matter Hiltner is now in a position to offer his own definition of pastoral theology:

Pastoral theology is defined as that branch or field of theological knowledge and enquiry that brings the shepherding perspective to bear upon all the operations and functions of the church and the minister, and then draws conclusions of a theological order from reflection on these observations.[10]

We may note that Hiltner is arguing for an *inductive* rather than a *deductive* approach to practical theology. Instead of the other theological disciplines laying down the norms for understanding the practical functions, Hiltner is suggesting that the study of the practical functions will produce some theological insights.[11]

These brief summaries of Hiltner's and Thurneysen's theories may have served to draw attention to some of the contrasts between them. It is very clear that they approach the definition of practical theology from opposite ends of the theological spectrum. Consequently each approach provokes its peculiar set of problems. Thurneysen's definition locates practical theology firmly within the framework of scripture, tradition and the ongoing preaching of the Gospel. In such an analysis practical theology is bound to be subservient to biblical and historical theology, the ground on which it stands being identical with that of these two disciplines. Yet we might question whether the very coherence of Thurneysen's position has not meant an undesirable narrowing down of the understanding of the mission of the church. Preaching, understood primarily as verbal communication, has been given such a normative position that the call of the church to heal and serve the needy, the poor and the outcast[12] finds no clear place; moreover it must be asked whether the *koinonia* of those gathered in Christ's name can be adequately understood in a purely kerygmatic context. Again, Thurneysen's insistence on membership of the church as a precondition or an indispensible goal of pastoral care rules out the possibility that God may be at work outside the church as well as within it. In short, Thurneysen buys coherence and consistency at too high a price. The categories of verbal communication and adherence to church membership confine too narrowly the potential scope of practical theology.

Quite another set of problems arises from Hiltner's approach to the subject. He is very concerned to earth theology in the human sciences and to allow the insights of contemporary experience in general, and of the counselling situation in particular, to revitalize the church's understanding of its task. Thus practical theology accepts concepts from depth psychology, sociological theory and group dynamics, since they all contribute to the fresh theological understanding that can come from the operation centred fields. It is strange how unaware Hiltner seems to be of the fundamental methodological problems which his definitions create. His division of the body of divinity into logical and operational fields hardly solves the basic problem of how the present experience of the church is related to its historical basis as attested to in scripture. Indeed the division he proposed severely deepens the cleavage between the two.[13] Again his theology seems to have no place for the category of revelation – even in the negative sense of deliberately espousing 'natural theology'. It simply ignores all the questions to do with historicity and uniqueness. A fellow American theologian has acutely characterized the theological inadequacy of Hiltner and many of his followers:

> If revelation at least remains a live issue for Tillich and Thurneysen, it hardly seems to be a vital problem in the American tradition of pastoral care, which in the footsteps of Ritschl, Troeltsch and Harnack has thought it could proceed quite as well without the excess baggage of Nicaea, Chalcedon, etc. It has been content to derive its 'theological' bearings essentially from psychological case studies and clinical pastoral relationships, the results of which is a *derivative* or functional theology, in which theology *functions* now and then to help out in the solution of some practical problem.[14]

More surprising still is Hiltner's implicit assumption that the 'operations' of the church are a kind of given from which practical theology may begin. By bringing different perspectives to bear (the shepherding, the communicating, etc.) on these operations new theological truth is to be gained. Yet surely what the churches and their ministers are, or do, at any given time or place is bound to be sociologically and culturally conditioned to a very large extent. It is hardly a place from which to *begin* theologizing from whatever perspective. The very *existence* of the churches needs a theological justification and what their ministers *do* is open to more radical questioning than simply whether they are effective communicators, organizers and pastors. There is no place in Hiltner's definition of the practical disciplines for a radical theological critique of the churches in the light of a question like Bonhoeffer's celebrated self-interrogation in prison: 'What is bothering me incessantly is the question what Christianity really is, or indeed who Christ really is, for us today.'[15] We can find in Hiltner an ecclesiastical conservatism more profound (because less open to theological correction) than that of Thurneysen.

Our investigation to this point has led to a negative answer to the question about the possibility of an independent and viable practical theology. The type of definition proposed by Thurneysen effectively subsumes the subject under dogmatic theology whilst the formulations of Hiltner, despite his admirable intentions, leave the subject in the limbo of pragmatism. It would be audacious to suppose that some new and original solution could now be offered which will avoid the criticisms made of previous viewpoints. Yet a hint of a solution may be gained from the persistent re-appearance of the problem of church-centredness which has been evident in one form or another since the first definition by Schleiermacher. It seems that the articulation of the nature of practical theology is intimately related to one's understanding of the relationship between the life of the church and the life of the world 'outside the church'. Practical theology's concern for operations and its relatedness to specific situations needs to be grounded in some systematic conceptualization of the church-world relationship.[16]

One begins the quest for re-definition, then, by asking why the things that are done by Christians are done, and what their relationship is to the things done by non-Christians. (Put in another way, one does *not* accept the functions of church and ministry as given.) An answer to this can be given in the following terms: the actions of Christians are celebrations of and attestations to God's reconciling work in the world which begins and ends in Jesus Christ. The relationship of these actions to those of non-Christians is one of both similarity and difference. The similarity is that *all* human actions both participate in and fall short of the purposes of God. The difference is that those who profess belief and adhere to membership of the church have been called to *make explicit* the celebration of God's work.

This understanding of the nature of the church was elaborated in a World Council of Churches report on evangelism published in 1967:

Since God is constantly active in the world and since it is his purpose to establish *shalom*, it is the Church's task to recognize and point to the signs of this taking place. The Church is always tempted to believe that the activity and presence of God are confined within the boundaries it draws round itself and to think that *shalom* is only to be found within them. But the whole world was implicated in the death and resurrection of Christ. Hence everything in the world may have a double aspect. Each time a man is imprisoned, tortured or destroyed, death is at work. But each time a man is a true neighbour, each time men live for others, the life giving action of God is to be discerned ... So God, as he moved towards his final goal, is using men and women, both inside and outside churches, to bring signs of *shalom* ... What else can the churches do than recognize and proclaim what God is doing in the world?[17]

The emphasis in this report on 'what God is doing in the world' was a familiar one in the new explorations in theology of the 1960s. It reflected reactions to the 'death of God' and the 'secular theology' debates, and it found a particularly strong expression in the writings of Joseph Fletcher, J. A. T. Robinson and Paul Lehmann.[18] Since that era things have moved on in the theological debate. There is now more awareness of the radical political implications of the theology which takes the notion of a historically active God seriously. The 'option for the poor' of political theology generally and of liberation theology in particular has presented a challenge to the whole ideological foundation of Western theology and biblical scholarship. We are now so far removed from the seemingly secure ecclesiastical world of Thurneysen and Hiltner that there is surely no way back to an uncritical 'churchiness' in practical theology. At the same time the liberal optimism of the 1960s with its confidence in secular institutions is also radically under question. The new agenda for practical theology must therefore be both politically aware and theologically courageous. Religious language is not to be swept aside by simplistic translations into secular alternatives, but when religious imagery is used, it must be subjected to the acid test of a relevance, beyond a personalist salvation, to a social and political renewal. This is the inescapable atmosphere within which one must attempt a practical theology today.

Against the background of these challenges facing practical theology, we may now sketch out a re-definition of its nature and scope.

1. Practical theology is concerned with the study of specific social structures and individual initiatives within which God's continuing work of renewal and restitution becomes manifest. These may be found either inside or outside the life of the church.

2. Practical theology can no longer take the functions of the ordained ministry as normative for its divisions of subject matter and delineation of scope. The ordering of the fellowship of believers is of concern to the practical theologian, but only as part of the wider question of the place of the witnessing, serving and loving community within the whole economy of salvation. A consequence of this is that instead of 'missions' and 'acts of charity' being seen as peripheral to the scope of the discipline, they move into the centre of its concern. If a division of subject matter is necessary at all, it may perhaps be found in the three-fold nature of the church's life – *kerygma, koinonia, diakonia* – provided always that these are understood in ways that open the church to the world.[19]

3. The relationship between practical theology and the other theological disciplines is *neither inductive* (cf. Hiltner), *nor deductive* (cf. Thurneysen). The relationship is to be seen as a 'lateral' rather than a 'linear' one. Practical theology juxtaposes concrete situations of witness, celebration and service with the findings and formulations of the biblical, historical and philosophical subjects in the theological corpus. It does this not in order to correct according to some canon of relevance, nor in order to be corrected according to some canon of orthodoxy. It is more an exercise in creative imagination, the interplay of idea and action, with all the ambiguity and inconclusiveness which this implies.[20]

4. Because of the 'situation-based' method it employs, practical theology can be expected to be fragmentary and poorly systematized. If it is constantly seeking out and presenting newly emerging situations, it cannot at the same time present a comprehensive and coherent account of itself. (Yet in this respect it perhaps differs only in *degree* not in *kind* from the other theological disciplines where the constantly increasing volume of research and proliferation of alternative theories militate against a statement of a 'position' which will not subsequently be questioned.)

5. The 'findings' of practical theology can be expected to be mostly the form of *concrete proposals* for the re-structuring of the church's life of witness, fellowship and service, for the style of life of individual Christians within the 'secular' structures of society, and for the renewal and reforming of the secular structures themselves.[21] At the same time such proposals must then become the subject of fresh theological reflection if practical theology is not to return to a new form of 'hints and tips', but one with a fashionable political emphasis. The discipline must remain a critical one, and this it can achieve by retaining its relationships with the other disciplines in the theological corpus. There can be no excuse for a practical theology based on an outmoded biblical theology, or on a poorly reasoned set of theological categories. Practical relevance must never be equated with an unreflective pragmatism lacking in self criticism and historical perspective.

This brief survey of the recent history of practical theology has suggested that the subject must be re-defined if it is to be re-instated as a viable branch of theological study. The re-definition proposed sets it the task of selecting contemporary situations from the life of the church and the world and setting them alongside the current theories and research conclusions of biblical scholars, church historians and systematic theologians. This in turn generates proposals for action which create fresh situations for study. Such a definition is designed to give practical theology a method and momentum of its own which sets it apart from the other branches of theology, whilst articulating its relationship to them. It is an attempt to create a discipline which is both practical and critical.

But it would be naive to suppose that the case for the possibility of practical theology now rests proven. An obvious weak spot in the definition may at once be identified: On what criteria is one to select the 'concrete situations' for study and experiment especially when these are to come from outside as well as inside the life of the church? Do practical theologians have the temerity to suggest that they can discern where God is at work, say in international politics, or in the works of writers and artists, or in the dilemmas of modern technological society?

Perhaps one must answer that such boldness *is* indeed required. In an age when destruction seems ever closer at hand – whether from environmental degradation, world political unrest, the crippling social problems of 'developed' societies, the debilitation of world hunger and increasing poverty, or the ending of it all in nuclear holocaust – it seems that *some* branch of theology must be concerned with matters which directly affect human well-being in whatever future awaits us. This appears to be a task especially suited to a re-created 'practical theology', one which treads a difficult path between practical relevance and theological integrity.

Nevertheless the possibility of such a practical theology is only minimally established. It is only in the implementation of the kind of objectives that this essay had proposed that the discipline can either establish its viability, or join its nineteenth-century predecessor on the scrap heap of old confusions.

3

The Bible and Christian Practice

J. Ian H. McDonald

The relationship of the Bible to Christian practice is problematic. Some Christians may feel that it ought not to be so. The Reformed tradition, after all, focusses on the Word revealed in scripture. Christian practice must therefore be a response to the Word. The difficulty lies in the particularity of given situations. The Word does not supply a direct and unequivocal answer to all the dilemmas of Christian moral practice. Indeed, the attempt to encapsulate the divine requirement in dogmatic rules or formulae and to apply these to specific situations tends to foreclose discussion of the issue: the answer is given before the question is heard! Wisely, the tradition of moral theology takes the Bible as a general guide only. 'The scriptures cannot be used as a proof text for a very specific moral conclusion which is often arrived at on other grounds.'[1] But how do you use the Bible in relation to specific situations? Has it anything to say to me when I am confronted with a personal dilemma or a question of social or political policy?

A helpful way to approach the problem may be to ask: what is involved in *reading* the Bible today? Let it be stated unequivocally that we cannot separate 'Bible' from reading or interpreting the Bible. The Bible comes to us as a written book or books, and all reading is essentially a process of interpretation. There is no direct access otherwise provided; no 'plain unadorned meaning' that discounts engagement with the text.

Perhaps, however, this is a description of our embarrassment, for the Bible is not only a complex and varied document, it is also an ancient document far removed from today's scientific and technological culture. Yet this is not an insuperable problem. It is an exaggeration to claim, as some have done, that historical epochs are like hermetically sealed containers housing wholly different products. Human beings of all societies inhabit a world; live and die and reflect on life and death; reside in families or communities and carry out certain roles within them; have their beliefs and doubts, hopes and fears ... In short, human existence is a common factor, however different the 'worlds' which people inhabit may be. Traditions – religious and cultural – also provide links over the centuries. Reading and understanding ancient texts, though demanding, are by no means impossible or hopeless tasks. If it had been so, the Bible would possibly never have come into being in the first place!

There are, of course, other difficulties which militate against a reflective reading of the Bible. A fast moving society demands quick, if not instant, answers to problems. Communication today tends to be about data and the availability of data. We have data banks, computer records with instant access, news in neat capsules. Information is skilfully summarized for instant digestion. Analysis may follow, but it is also carefully packaged and seldom particularly demanding. Information and news must have impact. Reaction rather than reflection is the preferred response. In such an age, answers to moral and spiritual problems are also expected to be instant. The wayside pulpit, the 'daily text', and the Gideon Bible go some way towards meeting this demand, and while some good may come of them they are not an adequate approach to understanding the Bible and practice. Now we even have 'dial a text'! The Authorized Version, with its memorable individual verses, may have contributed to the fascination with snippets, but cultural forces today are probably much stronger factors. Finally, there is the pulpit text: often treated in isolation and sometimes a virtual pretext for homiletic musings rather than a furthering of biblical understanding.

It is against this background that it is suggested here that we need to learn, or re-learn, how to read the Bible and encounter the Word which it may convey to us. The Bible comes to us as testimony. It bears witness to God through his relationship with his people, who in turn bear testimony to his ways and his wisdom. It is important not to be too fascinated with its printed form. The printed page, so efficient for fast dissemination, is but an invitation to receive the witness, discern the Spirit and hear the Word. It is a pointer to the living reality of God's message, and to its power to illumine, convict and transform. What then is involved in the process of reading? How can we take the book, read and learn? And how may this act influence our practice?

Reading the Bible

To read the Bible is to enter the world of the text. The text is an encoded message or symbolic statement. To decode and inter- pret it successfully requires more than knowledge of mere words or grammar or syntax. It requires us to imagine our way into the situation or world which the text is designed to open up for us. Texts operate in different ways depending on their genre: whether they are, for example, poems or historical narratives or parables or letters. We must recognize the kind of material which the text presents to us and then allow ourselves to be drawn into its discourse.

Let us take as an example the parable which Nathan told David. The situation was, of course, a living, personal en- counter. Nathan *told* the story to David; David did not read it. Obviously, elements such as voice and body language enter into this kind of communication in a way that does not apply to written discourse. Nevertheless, the presentation of the story provides an excellent example of how narrative or parabolic material may draw one into the world that it creates for the receptor (hearer or reader) and how the latter may subcons- ciously resist the challenge of the material.

'There were two men in a certain city, the one rich and the other poor' (II Sam. 12.1). One builds up a picture of them in their contrasting worlds: the rich man with his abundant flocks and herds; the other with his one ewe lamb which he and his household, in their poverty, prized and cherished. Step by step, the hearer is inducted into the pathos of the situation: 'it used to eat of his morsel, and drink from his cup, and lie in his bosom, and it was like a daughter to him' (12.3). Our sympathy is engaged: our emotions endorse the idyll. Then the action – the plot – moves on. The arrival of an unexpected guest prompts the rich man, unwilling to reduce his prime flock, to avail himself of the poor man's ewe lamb for the purposes of the feast. The more deeply we have empathized with the story, the greater our outrage as we imagine the sense of loss and sorrow occasioned to the poor man and his household. In the narrative of II Samuel, it is David who gives expression to the hearer's moral outrage. He passes judgment on the rich man, as he is accustomed to do as king, and requires four-fold restitution, 'because he did this thing, and because he had no pity' (12.6).

So far, so good. We note that when David allows himself to react as king and judge, he is effectively defending himself from further personal involvement in the story. His own personal life – the question of whether he resembles the rich man – is kept out of the picture. The defensiveness of the receptor is therefore a factor in biblical interpretation. When one aspect of the biblical message – whether an isolated text or, as here, a single perspective – is accepted for personal reasons as the whole picture, it has the effect of excluding or diluting other aspects of the message.

However, the written narrative we have in II Samuel not only presents the story which Nathan told David; it also describes the context in which the story was told and the consequence of Nathan's encounter with David. We have read of David's cruel, selfish and immoral action in bringing about the death of Uriah and acquiring Bathsheba as his wife (II Sam. 11.2–27). We have read of the divine displeasure and understand that Nathan the prophet has been commissioned to deliver the 'word of the Lord' to David. We are therefore aware that the story has a reference beyond the characters active in its plot, the anonymous rich man, poor man and traveller. In other words, we as readers know that the story is a parable. We note the irony of the situation when David identifies with the story in such a way that he can pronounce a royal judgment on the deed. Such is his personal insensitivity that Nathan has to confront him with the reality of his behaviour. He does so with the words 'You are the man' (12.7) – the most dramatic sentence in the Old Testament.

As David absorbs this statement with (we may imagine) a mixture of resentment and fury, Nathan conveys to him an interpretation of his actions from God's point of view, for he was commissioned to convey the word of God. This has the effect of undermining David's defences, cancelling any royal prerogative he might have wished to appeal to and revealing him as a sinner in the sight of God.

The narrative which includes Nathan's parable demonstrates how one may enter the world of the text. It is clear that David did enter the world of the story, but on his own terms. It took something of a prophetic *tour de force* to enable him to encounter the story in a new way and find a new understanding of himself in the process. For him, the story came as a parable to have a disconcerting and world-shattering power. Personal renewal came later.

Reading, therefore, involves entering the world of the text and appreciating its plot or action. It involves discerning the nature of the text: is it, for example, a case study put to David for judgment, or a parable involving David's own conduct? It entails opening oneself to the text, so that one's own cherished presuppositions and rationalizations may be brought into question. In this way, the text involves one in the issue under discussion (the rhetorical issue). The context of the passage is not simply its setting in II Samuel or its historical milieu, though both are important. There is also a wider context which includes the reader and which involves him or her in the rhetorical issue. Hence, the passage may leave us contemplating how we exercise power over others, whether we exploit or manipulate others or whether we treat them with integrity and compassion. It may also cause us to reflect on how power is exercised, or should be exercised in society; not least, on the place of moral constraint, and how it can become effective.

To read the Bible is to be more than a student of ancient literature or a detached observer of the action portrayed. Reading is an act of commitment to the text. To encounter the Bible is to allow ourselves to be drawn into the discourse, to be challenged by it and to be changed by it. It is to read it as a contemporary message, as a Word addressed to us. In short, it means to read it in the context of personal and practical concern.

To say this is to reaffirm the tradition of Bible reading throughout the ages. It may well be the case that, since the church has heard the Bible as a contemporary message in different epochs, interpretation in one age may seem strange to a later age: Augustine's interpretation of the parable of the Good Samaritan is a case in point. Yet that is not to suggest that his interpretation was wrong-headed or inauthentic, or that the Good Samaritan window in Chartres Cathedral is no more than a mythological fantasy. It is to recognize that the Bible must be approached today in ways appropriate to our situation. From the so-called Age of Enlightenment, a historical perspective has dominated interpretation, and has proved productive. Yet, if adhered to exclusively, this approach sharpens the 'two-worlds' view: ancient and modern, subject and object. Today, a new perspective is demanding attention, in science as in religion and literature. It is a holistic view, a participative approach to the reality of existence to which we all belong. Herein lies the prospect of encountering the biblical message in a fresh and exciting way, leading to nothing less than the transformation of thought and action.

The Bible in worship

Reflection on the use of the Bible in worship provides a useful confirmation of the interpretation of Bible reading given above. From relatively early times, some form of scriptural reading has found a place in Christian worship. Indeed, the Christian inheritance from the synagogue was rich in this respect. In synagogue worship, the community literally centred on the Torah. Not only did the reading or recitation of the scriptures occupy a focal position, but a homily was frequently given to assist the interpretation and appropriation of meaning. Lectionaries came to play an important part. The expositor selected a text which would throw light on the meaning of the prophetic passage for the day. Having achieved this object, he would then relate his discourse to the chief passage, which was of course from the Torah or books of Moses. The aim of the exercise was to enable the whole community to be brought to a new understanding of and a new obedience to the will of God.

It is likely that other Jewish practices influenced Christian worship. Sectarian movements about the time of Jesus tended to be messianic and eschatological in orientation. The best known examples are found at Qumran. Such communities believed that they had a special role in the new order which was about to be established as the fulfilment of the old. Hence, they believed, the scriptures spoke directly to them, interpreting their latter day vocation. Commentaries found among the Dead Sea Scrolls were written to interpret the meaning of the text for the sectarians. Their perspective is eschatological and immediate, not historical in orientation.

Christian interpretation of scripture draws on both of these

Jewish procedures. In a sense, all scripture testifies to Jesus as Messiah (cf. John 5.39). Christians therefore read the scriptures – Old Testament and New Testament alike – in the light of belief in Jesus as Christ. Christian interpretation therefore presupposes a kind of dialogue within the scriptures in which the interpreter is invited to join and through which the Bible as a whole speaks as the Word of God.

From early times, the ministry of the Word has been an essential part of worship. It may be thought of as an invitation to enter the world of the Bible. This is not simply an ancient world, inhabited by people like David and Nathan. The reading of the text opens up a rhetorical world which includes the worlds inhabited by the characters in the text and by the modern readers or hearers. In other words, through reflection on the passages from Old and New Testaments, issues are opened up which may challenge our presuppositions. It is the genius of prophetic or parabolic texts to encompass such a confrontation, to open up new possibilities for us, and to challenge us to respond to the address of God. 'Come now, let us reason together, says the Lord' (Isa. 1.18). The interaction of the texts in the lectionary contributes directly to the process, so that we more readily discern the voice of Christ, who may speak from the Old as from the New Testament. He may speak from the troubles and wrongheadedness of a disobedient people, as well as from the testimony of the saints. And in this converse of the Word, the sermon should play an enabling, rather than an obstructive part.

An extension of this type of thinking would lead us to describe the ministry of the Word as sacramental, just as the eucharist is sacramental. It is an encounter or involvement with a realm beyond ourselves which nevertheless communicates with us in worship and redirects our practice in the world. To return to David: his immediate response to the disclosure of his sinfulness might be sackcloth and ashes, but what he was actually called to do was to change his practice while enduring the consequences of his misdeeds. We are set in a historical context, which affects our scope for action and is affected by our deeds and misdeeds. It is unhistorical and unrealistic to think that repentance or forgiveness wipes the sheet clean! We still have to reckon with the consequences of our misdeeds, though the sense of being pardoned may give us strength for the task.

Objection might be made to this biblical understanding of

worship on the grounds that it reflects Reformed rather than Catholic thinking. This is not, in fact, the case. In the second century AD, the services in Justin's congregations began with the testimony of the prophets and the memoirs of the apostles.[2] Christian *anamnesis*[3] involves the recalling of the story of salvation, including the story of Jesus, as the Word which informs all Christian worship. In the ideal scheme of Hippolytus, the first step taken by catechumens was to become hearers of the Word.[4] Without undervaluing the role of confession of faith in worship, one might claim that the place of scripture in worship was greatly reduced when doctrinal propositions became the focus of belief and the reading of scripture became so stylized that it came to be read in a 'sacred' language no longer comprehensible to the worshippers. What was sacrificed was the opportunity to engage with the world which opens out in front of the text, potentially a much more existential engagement than doctrine or theology can offer precisely because it is expressed in human and personal terms, and in iconic language rather than abstract terminology.

A second objection perhaps has more force. Engagement implies reflection, dialogue, self-awareness, the development of a critical consciousness, and so on. In short, it implies discussion, the opportunity to explore possibilities and problems of responding to the gospel today. Little opportunity is given in modern churches – and particularly in modern worship – to discuss and explore the realms of meaning implicit in the service. The passionate engagement which was evident in ancient synagogue worship and in the tradition of the Stoic-Cynic diatribe was eventually submerged in the formalism of the *sermo* or oratorical monologue, which has persisted into modern times.[5] Gatherings for congregational fellowship after the service tend to offer only limited opportunity for discussing the substance of the sermon, let alone the scripture on which it is supposedly based. Discussion groups tend to involve only the few, while Bible study groups have usually a programme of their own. A practical step would be to inculcate greater awareness of the nature of worship and particularly the element of encounter with the Word.

A final qualification should be entered. Response to the Word is the response of the whole being, not simply the intellect. When speaking of understanding the scripture, one may give the impression of intellectual endeavour, but the response of the emotions and the will is no less important. In this matter of response, one touches upon intensely personal ground, a fact which suggests the essential interrelation of worship and pastoral care.

The Bible and pastoral care

There can be casualties. The Bible contains many powerful images, and the possibility of misusing them is always present. There are images relating to alienation, such as judgment and eternal punishment. There are images of warfare, such as slaughter of God's enemies. There are powerful religious images, such as Satan and demon possession, or the sin against the Holy Spirit. There are major pitfalls in interpretation, from non-contextual literalism to personal and individual revelation. It is relatively easy for people who are disturbed by some inner conflict or who are wounded or pressured in some way, to get hold of the wrong end of the stick and to emerge with a punitive or aggressive attachment to some aspect of scripture which represents something of a psychological block. The dialogue within scripture has been short-circuited or entered upon inadequately. The part has not been related to the whole, and the perspective upon the Bible has become warped. Perhaps the best assistance the pastor can give is to invite the persons concerned to talk about their views. To explore why such weight is being given to a selected verse or theme may offer a way into the seat of the pastoral problem.

The Bible also sets traps for the unwary pastor. The richness of the imagery and the intensity of religious emotion may induce the pastor to adopt short-cuts of various kinds and impose a solution upon a problem with which he or she has not come to terms or discussed helpfully with the person concerned. The range of operations involved in interpreting the Bible gives fair warning that any kind of 'automatic' or instant employment of biblical texts is likely to be unproductive. Such abuses have led some pastors to question whether the Bible has a place in pastoral counselling at all. This is very regrettable, for it closes off possibilities of using the Bible as a fundamental resource in situations of distress where the opening up of the world of the text might well offer healing, comfort and hope.[6]

The central point is that the Bible is essentially a witness to that which is true and authentic in the human situation. It points to a transcendent dimension expressed in history by many who walked with God, and definitively in Jesus Christ. The stories and symbols open up before us the prospect of hearing a true Word for our situation. They therefore find a place in a whole range of pastoral activity, as well as in funeral services and occasions of special stress. A moving example of this was provided by the memorial service for the victims of the Lockerbie air disaster, when a Pan American jumbo jet had crashed on this small town. The story of Lazarus was read as one of the lessons. The preacher began by citing the reproach of Martha: 'Lord, if you had been here, my brother would not have died.' The words summed up the agony of the town, its outrage at what had happened, its sense of helplessness and loneliness. The story spoke, in a way that propositions and doctrines could not. Gently, the preacher moved on to the Cross as the point at which human suffering was seen to be shared by God and turned towards hope.

The Bible and ethics

There is no space here for an extended discourse on the general theme of the Bible and ethics. Clearly, it is a complicated subject, demanding close attention to context and epoch. It is always important to relate the part to the whole, otherwise an imbalanced view may well emerge. And what was said above about the dialogue within scripture continues to have force. Yet the contemporary context of the reader is also important: we are not simply studying ancient history. In other words, the Bible may be read today in the context of ethical concern.

It is important to note that we stress here the *reading* of the Bible: i.e. engaging with a selected passage or passages. There is point, of course, in pinpointing certain summary rules (Ramsey) or central principle (Fletcher) to be applied to given situations. Here one would expect prominence to be given to *agape* and related concepts. In the New Testament, the double commandment of love has a summary function, as it had in a slightly different way in rabbinic debate. In Mark 12.28–34, the primary requirement is related not only to the acknowledgment of the One God (cf. Deut. 6.4f.) but also to the priority of the religio-ethical as compared to the cultic requirement. At least three levels of interpretation can be identified. One links with the prophetic criticism of the cult when divorced from moral action (cf. Amos). One relates to the debate between synagogue and temple circles in ancient Judaism about the place of the cult in the divine economy. The third raises the question of the relation of worship and moral action today. There is no question of *reducing* religious to moral requirement. Indeed, love to God is emphasized, but it is *inseparable* from the moral.

The parable of the Good Samaritan (Luke 10.25–37) greatly extends the thrust of the statement and engineers confrontation on the central issue. The argument about the cult is still reflected in the two temple characters who fail to carry out the moral requirement (i.e., priest and Levite). The procedure of the parable is to open out a situation in front of the text, which involves the hearers. The situation created involves an element of affront to the original audience. It is a Samaritan (an outsider, one of 'them' rather than 'us') who fulfils the Law. Yet the parable demands that the situation thus created be taken seriously and responded to. Jesus presses home the issue with a direct question based on the plot. The reluctance of the response is evident in the attempt to evade naming the Samaritan. And the audience, like the modern reader, is left to confront this direct challenge to the way one understands one's own world: to the demarcations that are so important to it, the rationalizations which oil its wheels, and the prejudices which provide the hidden curriculum.

Here one can perhaps reflect on the importance of the story for ethics. Summary rules and principles have their place, but New Testament ethics at its best finds expression in iconic representations of situations or events in which the human elements predominate and serve to delineate a real life issue. Hence, in Christian ethics worthy of the name, engagement with the text would seem to be of the essence of the project. It is too easy to take refuge in the categories of moral philosophy or abstract discourse, although one must acknowledge in full the importance of rational discussion. What is desirable is a balance of principle (or summary rule) and story, a unity of concept and image. The reader is thus helped to bring his or her story into dynamic interaction with the biblical material, not least as a challenge to basic presuppositions. Without the story which places one in a perspective that comes from beyond oneself, there is a danger of domesticating moral discourse, so that one remains in control of it. The discourse that reflects the divine requirement sets one, like David, under the judgment of God.

This insistence on the importance of the biblical input does not in any sense distance Christian ethics from the world of practice. At many points, it may be necessary to transpose Christian ethics into another key, for the business world or the world of politics is not usually open to direct biblical input! This, however, is a matter of communication rather than of substance. It may prompt analysis of the type of justice that is being presupposed in a given policy. The Christian should know clearly, for example, why a creative justice which reflects *agape* is to be preferred to an arithmetical justice (cf. a poll tax) which suits the well-off. The operation of story and parable fits well with a hermeneutics of suspicion which is ever on the look-out for the subterfuges of rationalization and the propaganda of those in power.

But is it reasonable to suggest that an ancient book like the Bible is relevant to the kind of issues which occur in the modern world: issues of which the biblical writers were completely unaware? The question is important, and may fittingly be addressed in our final section.

A test case for the Bible and ethics today

The implications of medical advances in the field of human fertilization and embryology were highlighted by the Report of the Warnock Committee, which considered the social, ethical and legal issues raised by such developments. Can the methods of biblical interpretation outlined above be of any service in an area which is so unrelentingly modern? The suggestion is made here that they can be, both as part of a 'hermeneutics of suspicion' which subjects modern authoritarian stances to critical scrutiny in the light of biblical perspectives, and as indicators of general moral direction. Such authoritarian stances may be of a religious or secular nature.

Central to the issue is the understanding of creation, presented in the Bible in story form. The creation motif, with its concept of the 'image of God' in man, suggests a high evaluation of human life. Equally strong is its emphasis on the stewardship of the created order, animate and inanimate. How is 'dominion' to be understood? Its primary connotation is that of 'rule' or 'authority' delegated to human beings by God: not unlike the 'rule' delegated to kings in Israel! The created order is not given to be abused or maltreated at the whim of fallible humanity. It is not given for exploitation or greed. It is a sacred trust given as a primary, moral concern. An implication of such a trust is that even the secrets of life itself are not set beyond the scope of human investigation. Equally, such new knowledge may only be applied for moral purposes. It may be observed in passing that this use of the creation stories is in no way anomalous. It is true to their symbolic nature that, when read in the context of modern ethical concern, they open up perspectives of understanding which are supremely relevant to modern dilemmas.

Now for the 'hermeneutics of suspicion'! One 'absolute' stance appeals to a modern form of 'natural law'. The created order, it is suggested, is governed by physical laws which are inviolable. Such laws discovered by science are no longer to be seen as essentially descriptive of 'the way things are' but prescriptive of the way they ought to be, for the nature of each organism is to seek its appropriate 'end' or fulfilment. Thus 'unwarranted' interference with inviolate physical laws is out of the question as a moral proposition. Yet it is clear that several fences are being rushed here. What does 'unwarranted' mean in this context? And even after Einstein's work, can one so glibly read off moral obligation from physical processes? It is as if God gave the created order to man and said 'Hands off!' Instead, he entrusted its cultivation and development to human stewards. The moral issue resides in their use or abuse of it.

Another view advanced to support the 'hands off' approach makes an appeal to the incarnation and therefore to the birth stories in the Gospels. The focus of attention is on the conception of Jesus by the Holy Spirit or the Virgin Birth. The argument is that such symbols rule out any 'tampering' with the process of human fertilization in embryo research or any other way. Yet the biblical stories are about a particular and rather special conception and birth. As Karl Barth has put it, 'there is no question of a sexual event ... This procreation was realized rather by way of the ear of Mary, which heard the Word of God.'[7] In other words, the basis of the attempted analogy is defective. Such narrow interpretations of the incarnation are unsuited to the justification of 'absolute' ethical stances of this kind.

To reject the misuse of biblical images is by no means tantamount to disowning all restraint in this field. Such restraints are not always welcomed — and are therefore all the more important — in a field in which some practitioners tend to suggest that it is permissible to make up the moral rules as they go along! Oliver O'Donovan graphically described Paul Ramsey's disconcerting encounter at a Washington symposium on *in vitro* fertilization. In reply to well argued ethical critiques, one doctor raged: '"I accuse Paul Ramsey of taking an ethical stance that is about one hundred years out of date and one that is totally inapplicable to meet the difficult choices raised by modern scientific and technological advance. Dogma that has entered biology either from Communist or Christian sources has done nothing but harm."'[8] The misuse in past or present of dogma can be a liability. It can provide the unsympathetic with material for scoring points in debate. Notice how the rhetoric of the objector attempts not only to discredit Ramsey's arguments as antiquated and irrelevant – without answering them! – but suggests that modern advances somehow require a modern ethics which arises out of the same culture. Ethics would then be an internal discussion within the closed world of the discipline which gave rise to the problem in the first place. Such a position is to be rejected, although it is necessary for ethics to relate adequately to the field in question. Ethics opens out on to the question of human values, which are everybody's concern. And Christian ethics, with its riches of symbol and story, is particularly well equipped to demonstrate the limits to experiment where fundamental values are being infringed.

The forbidden trees of the Garden represent depth symbols of human limitation or finitude. Human beings are not gods, nor may they act as such. Good and evil are not simply human conventions but have a transcendent aspect. Answers to moral problems, including those raised by scientific and technological advance, must therefore be sought within the moral realm, however inconvenient the process may be to researchers or practitioners. The new advances do not move the moral goal posts! On the other hand, the potentiality of research to enrich the human lot and to take humanity forward into a new phase of the stewardship of creation must be recognized. Too often, religious sentiment merely harks back to an earlier, simpler period, like the Rechabites in the Old Testament. Yet the movement of the biblical story is forwards into the unknown future that is God's gift, to be accepted in faith and obedience, and with the hope of liberation. This is the story which provides the biblical context that informs the formal ethical operations in Christian ethics: operations such as the application of *agape* as summary role or principle and the casuistry or debate involving the 'facts of the case'. Christian ethics is never *simply* moral philosophy. It includes, but has a wider range than, moral argumentation. It sets the given issue in the context of human historicity and finitude. Theologically, it views *homo sapiens* as creature in the presence of Creator. And its main instrument for doing so is the Bible opening out upon practice.

Certainly there is no scope here for a detailed analysis of the issue of *in vitro* fertilization.[9] Our aim has been to indicate how a biblical perspective informs the approach to the question, while avoiding the pitfalls of dogmatic misuse of texts and symbols and resisting the professional closed shop. In this way, one may create a theologically informed context of moral concern within which the issue may be properly reviewed. And such a context is essential, even if it has to be justified in terms of principles or summary rules, for it is not moral to permit such practices solely in terms of market forces or simply because the technology is in place. Fundamental questions about personal values or the value of life must be raised. Christian ethics is in a position to give a lead here rather than simply to follow a trend, whether modernist or traditional. The issue can be explored as a possible life-enhancing enrichment of the created order. Only if it passes that test can we expect God to look upon it and declare that it is good.

II

Theology and Society

4

Towards a Theology of Peace

J. Ian H. McDonald

Like a good wine, this article has been maturing for a number of years. Whether it is palatable depends on its intrinsic quality, of which the reader must be the judge. It had its origins in a series of lectures on 'War and Peace' which I was invited to give to US army chaplains at Augsburg, West Germany, in the spring of 1983. It was further shaped by an invitation to address the CANA Conference (Clergy Against Nuclear Arms) at Dunblane, Scotland, in December of the same year. Thereafter, it lay inert in my files or perhaps maturing in my mind until an opportunity might present itself for producing it for general consumption.

Meanwhile, much was happening to change the interface of the Super Powers. In my original discussion of deterrence, I had looked for an initiative from the West. In fact, it came from the East. The Gorbachev era inaugurated hitherto unthinkable changes within the USSR and suggested unprecedented opportunity in international relations. At the time of writing, hopes are higher than expectations: that Gorbachev will be able to maintain the work of reform in the Soviet Union; that the progress in eliminating classes of nuclear weapons and effecting arms reductions will be sustained; and that the West, inhibited as it appears to be by its post – World War II mind-set, may rediscover a moral purpose that outweighs its gross materialism and the policies that go with it. One reflects on how quickly the international situation has changed, and may change again. A test of an article such as this is how far it can maintain credibility in the context of this rate of change. It was never intended as an ephemeral tract but as a consideration of principle. It may be regarded as an illustration or expression of the kind of interpretative approach spelled out in my chapter on 'The Bible and Christian Practice'. It is an attempt to read the biblical message of *shalom* in the context of concern for peace in the world today and to engage in critical dialogue with contemporary political thinking on that basis.

The concept of peace: 'Shalom'

The root meaning of the 'iridescent'[1] term *shalom* is 'wholeness', 'total soundness', even 'integrity'. It is close to the modern term, 'fulfilment'. It denotes a flourishing state of personal well-being, health, even prosperity; but as no man is an island, this well-being cannot be separated from social or corporate well-being, community or fellowship: the latter being expressed notably in 'the covenant of peace'. Indeed, this corporate understanding is clearly a major element in the concept of *shalom*, which is also interwoven with the notion of salvation itself. Both are gifts of God. And the peace he gives embraces his whole creation: 'the beasts of the field, the birds of the air, and the creeping things of the ground' (Hosea 2.18). The Psalmist puts it memorably:

> Let me hear the words of the Lord:
> are they not words of peace,
> peace to his people and his loyal servants
> and to all who turn and trust in him?
> Deliverance is near to those who worship him,
> so that glory may dwell in our land.
> Love and fidelity have come together;
> justice and peace join hands.
> Fidelity springs up from earth
> and justice looks down from heaven.
> The Lord will add prosperity,
> and our land shall yield its harvest.
> Justice shall go in front of him
> and the path before his feet shall be peace
> (Ps. 85.8–13, NEB).

If *shalom* relates to concepts such as love, fidelity, justice and salvation (all of them interrelating in the totality of soundness and integrity), the opposite syndrome, so often the lot of

disobedient Israel, comprises 'defeat, disunity, distrust, alienation, poverty and misery'.[2] War belongs to this scene: one can
speak of the *shalom* of the war, i.e., how the war was prospering
(II Sam. 11.7). To be a historical people – indeed, to be 'God's
people, Israel' in the harsh world of historical reality – entailed
involvement in the cut and thrust, the violence and bloodshed,
of international relations as they existed at that time. The
Old Testament does not lack realism in its awareness of the
'primitive' state of man and society. Of course, Israel prayed and
worked for victory: for anyone not to do so would have been to
incur the charge of disloyalty, as Jeremiah found to his cost.
Israel would have liked to have maintained a simple theodicy:
faithfulness to Yahweh brings success, unfaithfulness brings
defeat. But the nation came to know the recurring horror of
defeat, suffering and loss, and the need for a new theodicy.
Weary of conflict, Israel longed for *shalom* as 'rest from toil'.[3] In
the midst of wars and rumours of wars, people were ready to
share the vision of peace, when Yahweh 'will break bow and
sword and weapon of war and sweep them off the earth, so that
all living creatures may lie down without fear' (Hosea 2.18).
Weapons of war will be converted to peaceful uses:

> nation shall not lift sword against nation
> nor ever again be trained for war,
> and each man shall dwell under his own vine,
> under his own fig-tree, undisturbed.
> For the Lord of Hosts himself has spoken
>   (Micah 4.3f.,NEB).

Defeat and strife bring not only pain and exhaustion, they also
bring a sense of desolation, the reverse of flourishing – a sense
of being cut off from Yahweh, the source of *shalom*. And there is
no hint in the Old Testament that the state of complete fulfilment portrayed by the visions of *shalom* can readily be achieved,
or can be achieved at all, in this fragmented and disfigured
cosmos. The rise of the various expressions of messianic hope
testifies to the longing for a decisive divine action that would
renew and console Israel by re-establishing the reality of *shalom*
as the condition of those at one with their God, their neighbour
and their world.

The New Testament focusses on the healing of the alienation
between God and mankind. In the Christmas story, the angels
sing of *shalom* renewed on earth. Into the disfigured *cosmos* came

Jesus, healer and liberator, of whom the writer to the Ephesians could say, 'He is our peace' (Eph. 2.14). But this 'peace-making' entailed a radically new theodicy, even if it is foreshadowed in some prophetic strands of the Old Testament. The necessary paradox was that the One who embodied and activated *shalom* in a disordered world also brought into play the sword of opposition and conflict (cf. Luke 2.34f.). Rejected by the city 'that did not know the things that pertained to its peace', the climax of his ministry was the disfiguration of the Cross; yet this disfiguration was for our *shalom*' (Is. 53.5b) — 'the chastisement of our peace was upon him' (AV) The benediction of the disfigured One is, 'Peace be with you'. Though still rejected by the *cosmos* which does not recognize the extent of its bondage to the powers of alienation, something of the reality of Christ's *shalom* remains with all who discern in him the One who has broken down the iron curtain of hostility and made possible a new health, wholeness and fulfilment. And since this *shalom* is the gift of God to his creation, it redefines 'God's people' as the faithful community that transcends the boundaries of nationhood and race. This new community, founded on 'the stone which the builders rejected', constitutes 'a chosen race, a royal priesthood, a holy nation, a people for his possession', enjoying anew the 'mercy' of God (I Peter 2.9f.).

But how are we to interpret this theology? Does it mean that the action of God in Christ has resulted in a sort of private deal between God and the sect of the Christians, who can henceforth celebrate their salvation while the world goes on its heedless way to destruction? Not so, says Paul. The whole creation has been groaning in travail, a travail shared by the Christians, who have 'the first fruits of the Spirit', but do not yet know 'the redemption of our bodies' (Rom. 8.22f.). Such hope is integral to salvation, but hope implies 'not yet'. Hence, the church lives and moves in the 'relative' world, the world that is 'subject to futility' and in 'bondage to decay' (Rom. 8.20f.). Yet even that world experiences the longing for a different order of things, though its longing is without assurance or real hope. This is where the contribution of the church and its theology lies. For the faithful community knows that 'the Spirit helps us in our weakness' (Rom. 8.26), that the Spirit affords a foretaste of the *shalom* that is to be (cf. Rom. 8.23), and that 'in everything God works for good with those who love him' (Rom. 8.28). Hence the Christian hope is more dynamic than its Old Testament counterpart. The alienation between God and his creation has been overcome in Jesus Christ. A new dynamic has been launched, at the cost of the Cross: a dynamic that works for *shalom* within the travailing world and that will finally accomplish its purpose, for it is God's dynamic. Christians must not underestimate the futility to which the world is subject. They must not disengage from it in order simply to 'see visions and dream dreams'. But while recognizing the realities of the world situation, they must not become prisoners to it. They share its sufferings but not its bondage: and in the perspective of faith, these sufferings are the birth-pangs of a new age, an age already conceived in the ministry, death and resurrection of Jesus and slowly but surely gestating in the cosmic womb. Hence, since the church as the community of faith is sensitive to the 'signals of transcendence', it must relay its faith and hope to a world which has its own longings to transcend its bondage. It must relay the 'absolutes' that proceed from the fuller picture, but do so in a way that is credible within the limitations of the 'relative' world which sees its travail as the sign of death rather than of new and eternal life.

Our discussion has brought us from the concept of *shalom* to the means of applying it in the modern world. It is now time to take a closer look at this problem, which seems to fall into two parts: 1. Can we express the 'absolute' imperatives – '*shalom* whatever the consequences!' – in relation to the particularities as they arise? 2. Can we relate to the exigencies of particular situations as they arise on the political scene without betraying the goal of *shalom* and lapsing into 'double-talk'?

Shalom as means and end

We begin by considering two classic themes from the New Testament.

1. 'Blessed are the peacemakers, for they shall be called sons of God.'

The main thrust of this beatitude is 'the non-militant character of the true disciples of the Kingdom'.[4] The 'sons of the living God', in Hosea 1.10, is the name given to the redeemed Israel, who had previously been termed 'Not my people' because of their forsaking of God's ways. God's ways are taken by those who create *shalom*: who, in the words of James, reap the harvest of 'righteousness' that grows from seeds sown in a spirit of peace (James 3.18). It is thus that they enjoy the blessing of God. The non-militant emphasis can be deduced from the beatitudes in which Matthew places it: the peacemakers are also the pure in heart, the merciful, those who hunger and thirst for God's righteousness, and – significantly – those who are persecuted for the sake of it. But it is also in context with love to one's neighbour and, above all, love to one's enemy. In this respect, so far from Matthew's notion of peace representing a dilution of *shalom*, as K. Stendahl implies, it actually represents a fuller understanding of it than frequently appears in the OT. When Leviticus conceives the blessings of *shalom*, they include chasing your enemies and having them fall before you by the sword (Lev. 26.7). In Matthew the creators of *shalom* by their non-militancy avoid the demonization of their opponents, which is the hub of all war-policy, and make positive efforts to include the enemy within the circle of *shalom* (Matt. 5.43–48).

2. Turning the other cheek (Matt. 5.38–41)

As is well known, the basic saying is a radicalizing of the *lex talionis* (Ex. 21.24), which placed a restraint on vengeance. Jesus' radical interpretation and extension of this principle leads to the elimination of vengeance: non-retaliation and non-vindictiveness.

It is also clear that the primary *Sitz im Leben* of Jesus' teaching is life in an occupied country, in which violence was regularly offered to the subjugated people, a point illustrated by the Baptist's teaching to soldiers: 'Rob no one by violence or by false accusation, and be content with your wages' (Luke 3.14). The logic of Jesus' teaching is designed to avoid what would be called today an escalation of violence, as retaliation and vindictiveness would do. We might also say it has to do with absorbing aggression, with taking the heat out of the moment, with creating a new situation ... But what would the early Christians have made of it?

Matthew most probably thought of it in terms of the suffering servant. In Matt. 12.18–21, we find a *verbatim* citation of Isa. 42.1–4, set interestingly in the context of healing: creating wholeness, *shalom*. Even more apposite to the theme of non-violence is Isa. 50.4–9. The prophet, taught by God, expounds the response proper to faithful Israel: not one of rebellion but of submission to suffering caused by the aggressor; perhaps the historical Jeremiah is the model here. No matter how great the provocation, the true Israel does not respond violently:

'... the Lord God stands by to help me;
therefore no insult can wound me.'

The way of the true Israel is not that of physical force or violence, nor even of ostentation. Characteristic of it is respect for the weak and vulnerable, and trust in the final victory of God who gives hope to the world.

The other line of interpretation emerges in Rom. 12. The emphasis is once more on non-retaliation; vengeance is the prerogative of 'the Lord' (cf. Lev. 19.18 – converse of loving one's neighbour). But it is also linked with Prov. 25.21f.:

'If your enemy is hungry, give him bread to eat;
if he is thirsty, give him water to drink;
so you will heap glowing coals on his head,
and the Lord will reward you.'

The proverbial expression 'glowing coals' probably refers to an ancient Egyptian penitential ritual. The English gnomic equivalent would therefore be sackcloth and ashes: you will evoke in him a sense of shame that will change his conduct. Again, there is a strong conviction that evil can be overcome with good.

Can this exegesis of scripture relate directly to Christian *praxis* today? One of the most remarkable features of twentieth-century political resistance has been the manner in which the truth and power of this biblical concept has been rediscovered and given practical expression by people as different as Mahatma Gandhi, drawing on the Hindu tradition, and Martin Luther King from the deep South of the USA.[5] King certainly testified to the creative power of suffering, though perhaps he emphasized it at the expense of other important elements in his campaign, such as logical argument (he out-thought his opponents) and appeal to law (he could claim the support of the Constitution). He also appealed to the conscience of his opponents and shamed them by the moral quality of his case. It was through such 'conscientization' (to borrow a term from Paulo Freire)[6] that King could look beyond the conflict to renewed negotiations and reconciliation. One of King's basic convictions was that there must be a coherence of means and ends, and important theological perspectives emerge here. If the believing community truly lives in Christ and under the sovereignty of God, then its actions – whether conceived as means or ends – give expression to God's reign. In this respect, the church's ministry is at one with Jesus, in whose ministry the reign of God was 'realized', 'inaugurated' or 'adumbrated'. Means and ends acquire coherence, if not identity, in the service of the kingdom.

In Martin Luther King's approach, non-violence was linked to strength rather than weakness – strength to love.[7] It was linked with courage rather than cowardice – the courage to be true to oneself and one's calling. It was part of the discipline of faith.[8] Untypically for one of his Southern evangelical background, he committed himself to a political expression of the gospel.[9] Objections to his view usually follow a 'two-worlds' pattern and amount to the privatization of the gospel. How zealously politicians advocate that the Christian message belongs to the 'spiritual' sphere, that it finds its proper expression in 'songs of praise', prayer meetings and good works; above all, that it does not interfere with 'their' world – the hard world of political decision-making – nor challenge their values. The answer to this kind of advocacy is clear. It lies in the concept of *shalom*: the health of the whole being is incomprehensible except in relation to the renovation of the whole world with which humanity constantly interacts and by which it is shaped. It also lies in the question, 'Am I my brother's keeper?' And behind the clamorous rationalizations of a distorted humanity, there is the still small voice that whispers, 'I am'. It lies too in the command, 'Love your neighbour as yourself'. Martin Luther King recognized that any response to that command was inadequate unless it sought to remove the barriers of discrimination and prejudice, struggled for civil and political rights for all, and brought liberation to the oppressed in the material forms of job opportunities, housing, education and health care. A political expression for the gospel is inherent in the nature of the gospel of *shalom*.

The keynote of this political expression is Christian responsibility: accepting loving responsibility for the *shalom* of one's neighbour, while completely respecting his/her integrity. But surely, someone protests, this has always been seen as a Christian duty? What's so different about the 'politics of peace' today, apart from a new set of theological clichés? Two features are of particular importance. 1. The world in which we live is more and more seen to be the global village: even the cosmic village. Never before has mankind been so evidently affected by the interrelation of all the parts. Never before has the harmony — the well-being, the *shalom* of the whole global and cosmic picture been so important. 2. Scientific and technological research has not only tapped the mighty resources of creation in nuclear fission but has presented humanity with manifold possibilities of self-destruction and global destruction on a scale undreamed of in previous generations.

For these reasons, if not for others, a new kind of Christian theology and politics is essential today; and in response to the contemporary needs another strand of biblical understanding bursts into new meaning. In the creation story, God gave man the rule or dominion over the earth and all created things. It is a distorted view of this 'dominion' that interprets it as a licence to exploit, exhaust and tyrannize. In the Bible, the responsibility for exercizing rule or authority (e.g. kingship in Israel) is not lightly given. The ruler is God's vassal, bound by God's teaching and charged with exercizing his responsibility in the light of it. The same concept — even the same language occurs in the creation story.[10] Christian responsibility, therefore, embraces love and care for neighbour (and enemy) and also loving care for all aspects of the creation. Theology is now as bound up with the concerns of ecology, physics and economics as it is with ethics and other areas of *praxis*. Our policy, *in nuce*, must therefore be to pursue and express God's all-comprehending *shalom*.

The praxis of shalom

We can now give a tentative answer to one of the questions we posed above. It is not so much that the Christian policy is '*shalom* whatever the consequences!' but rather that one is impelled to create *shalom*, in so far as one can, whatever the circumstances, pressures or constraints. Such is the imperative expressed by the psalmist: 'seek *shalom* and pursue it' (Ps. 34.14); such is the way of divine wisdom: all her paths are *shalom* (Prov. 3.17). But the exigencies of the situation must be taken seriously. A theology of *shalom* is not an escape mechanism nor a panacea. One of the most striking features of Gandhi and Martin Luther King is the extent to which they engaged with the circumstances, pressures and constraints of their situation and were yet able to develop an effective political strategy which so evidently expressed *shalom*. As some of the New Testament writers indicate clearly (we will discuss them shortly), it is not always possible in the immediate situation to adopt a policy that so patently unites means and

ends. Think of the Christian in local government, contending
with severe financial cut-backs imposed from above and having
to take extremely difficult and compromising decisions about
where the cuts should be implemented. One may well resort
in such a predicament to 'middle axioms': acting with
responsibility, analysing situations and claims as fairly as
one can, being open to the cases presented, trying amid the
difficulties to lay the foundations of a better future ... It all
seems so *un*theological: the pragmatic appears to be the order of
the day − not to speak of party advantage. But if we really
understand our theology (and eschatology), the scenario has a
different aspect. We work in a world that is estranged from God
and divided within itself; yet we work with *shalom* as our
theological context. In all the compromising difficulties and
difficult compromises, we still express *shalom*: whether in the
relative detachment ('freedom') with which we interpret events,
the positive criticisms we make, the patience and forbearance
('suffering'?) we are called upon to show, the opportunities for
reconciliation we take, the willingness to accept our errors and
failures ... It is only within the overall context of *shalom* that
middle axioms are acceptable guides; for into these lifeless
generalizations the Spirit must breathe quickening life.

Like the early Christians, we today have to come to terms with
national and international politics. Among the questions the
early Christians grappled with were whether one should pay
one's taxes and honour to a regime for which one had little
sympathy, and how to deal with persecution and prejudice.
They were not required by circumstances to face the problem of
being drafted for military service: that came later.[11] Nor had
they to face the question of international war and peace: they
were far removed from participation in decision-making at that
level. Still less had they to contemplate nuclear war, although
they knew how to live 'in the last hour'. Some of the questions
they faced remain live issues for Christians in many countries;
but Christians today have also to come to terms with many issues
which their first-century counterparts, in their political and
religious setting, did not have to confront. The problem is how
we are to develop the *praxis* of *shalom* in these settings for
which guidelines are hard to find. Or, to repeat our question:
how do we relate to the exigencies of particular situations as
they rise on the political scene without betraying the goal of
shalom or lapsing into 'double-talk'? We take as test cases two

important issues in the politics of defence: deterrence and de-escalation.[12]

The praxis of peace

To formulate the political implications of the gospel in general terms is one thing. To have impact on the political situation is another. Here, the need is clearly for involvement and critical dialogue in far-reaching terms. If the gospel is not heard through priesthood (always the more domesticated branch), then it must be heard through prophecy. For the purposes of this paper, a few illustrations of Christian *praxis* must suffice.

1. *Deterrence*. Even by the criteria of the 'just war' (probably a much maligned doctrine), nuclear war and many forms of modern warfare are completely condemned, both in terms of *ius ad bellum* and of *ius in bello*. The one toe-hold is deterrence. Can this notion cohere with that of *shalom*? Rom. 13.1–6 and 1 Peter 2.13–17 (whatever their status: we cannot discount them simply because they are problematic) certainly accept the deterrent function of the state and sovereign: 'rulers are not a terror to good conduct but to bad' (Rom. 13.3, RSV). But these passages are simply exhorting Christians to political involvement to the extent of being good citizens of an imperial power that was in many respects alien to them. They must conscientiously support the good ordering of society and the powers that restrained the violent and criminal; they must pay their taxes and their respect. But these passages, like the dominical maxim about rendering to Caesar and God what is due to them (Mark 12.17 par.), cannot be made to apply in all cases. If governors are terrors only to bad conduct, why were Christians condemned and martyred? If Caesar makes a totalitarian claim not only upon what is his due but also upon what is due to God, then it is another part of the Romans 13/I Peter 2 syndrome that is activated: viz., Christian freedom (I Peter 2.16) and conscience (Rom. 13.5). If Christians may *in extremis* and on specific grounds of conscience defy the civil power (Calvin saw clearly the necessity to recognize the right of rebellion: he is followed today, significantly enough, by Beyers Naudé and Allan Boesak in South Africa), then Christians are bound by conscience to subject the policy of deterrence in a nuclear age to the strictest scrutiny.[13] It is not that deterrence is to be rejected in principle. The biblical passages tend to accept the principle. We might go further and

concede that, since international society is no less immoral than national society and works on the basis of self-interest and opportunism, the checks and balances that a deterrent policy provides must exist in an effective way. We simply lack political credibility if we do not accept this factor, and we would fall far behind the insights of Romans 13 and I Peter 2 in terms of political realism. But what *kind* of deterrent? One that continues to fuel the arms race and to divert great resources from the poorer countries? One that keeps the whole world on the knife-edge of calamity? One that depends for its effectiveness on first strike capability?

The reason that prompts the political strategist to answer 'yes' is that for him peace means the preservation of the *status quo*. It is, I suggest, inexcusable for Christians to accept this view, because it is clearly unsound theologically and would mean endorsing all the worst effects of the policies to which we have become accustomed.[14] Christians must think not in terms of the modern *pax Augusta* but in terms of *shalom*; and there is no way in which they can square the present Western position with seeking that end. It would involve having the means and the end totally out of cycle.

Unlike the writers of Romans 13 and I Peter 2, the problem we face today is not how to bring Christians into proper subservience to the state: it is how to deliver them from the bondage of their present subservience to it. It is no longer enough to argue, as some do, that we should maintain the present deterrence policy until the disarmament talks begin to show positive results: that point is now passed. It is not enough to single out first strike capability as the single unacceptable feature: the present deterrence policy cannot operate without it. Nor is it sufficient to argue that the *threat* of using such a deterrent is not in itself immoral, as if the moral acceptability of present policy rested on such nuances of casuistry.[15] The fatal flaw resides in the present concept or interpretation of deterrence. It is nothing short of betrayal for Christians to allow themselves to be programmed in their thinking by the powers that be. The contemporary crisis is such that Christians must declare that the traditional policy of deterrence is morally unacceptable and must undergo a radical and urgent change in nature, or they must run the risk of being no better than the court priests and false prophets of Israel who always prophesied what the sovereign authority wanted to hear.

2. *De-escalation.* A modern policy of deterrence would be congruent with *shalom* only if present levels of armaments, nuclear and otherwise, were substantially reduced and the basic logic of deterrence policy radically revised. It is a condemnation of post – World War II policies of deterrence that they have led to a continuing escalation of the nuclear arms race which has, in turn, long passed the point of justification by any reasonable criteria. The justification lies wholly in the acceptance of the international ball-game, the rules of which have been drawn up by the leading competitors themselves. It does not reflect an inevitable reality, but simply the way in which these powers have insisted upon seeing themselves. It is of little moment now to attribute particular degrees of blame to Stalin, Roosevelt, Churchill or their successors. Because of their mutual fears and suspicions, the cold war was launched and along with it the arms race, mutual demonization, the current impasse, and – it appears – the extension of the deadly war-game into space. The heart of the matter lies in the neurotic fear which capitalist countries have of communist designs on world dominion, and the neurotic fear communist countries have had of capitalist imperialism. If Christians cannot exorcize these demons, at least they can insist that both patients require treatment: they lack *shalom.* The unforgivable sin is for Christians to endorse one side or the other: e.g., the conventionally or residually religious over against the atheistic anti-Christ (or the reverse, if that is conceivable). It is a fair point to indicate that the arms race has been led by the West and responded to in kind by the East. It may be equally fair to suggest that a new initiative is required – preferably from the West, now that the East under Gorbachev has produced initiatives of its own; and the new initiative should be in the direction of de-escalating the arms race, taking full advantage of the overtures made by the other side. Thus the process of de-escalation would be maintained as one, but only one, element in the *praxis* of *shalom.* And since it would operate a step at a time, it would still be consistent with deterrence, which would be assuming progressively rational proportions.[16]

To complete our projected outline for a theology of peace, two further points require to be noted: they have to do with repentance and self-awareness.

3. *Repentance and judgment.* A prominent part of the subject-matter of theology is the theme of repentance (in the sense of the biblical term *shub,* i.e., change of direction), renewal,

transformation, resurrection, hope. It is through experience of this kind that we grow in *shalom* and towards *shalom*. A movement of the nations in this direction is the presupposition of any meaningful de-escalation. It is also essential to the implementation of (for example) the Brandt report and to a proper sharing and conserving of the earth's resources. Nations *can* change direction: the ban on aerial testing of atomic weapons is a case in point. Nations can and do respond to what is in their own interests, and sometimes these interests are also those of humanity. A sense of *shalom* is given to all people. To be sure, it is distorted and manipulated by self-interest; but set in global perspective, the self-centred concern for survival may lead to a recognition of interdependence and to the first tentative steps towards global solidarity and health. But moves in this direction presuppose a shaking of present foundations: a measure of de-stabilization of the *status quo* so that a positive change of direction can occur.

Without such a change of direction, there is judgment. Even without the aid of the American film industry or biblical apocalyptic, we know the form that judgment may take. Until recently, many people – including the young – believed that judgment to be inevitable. After the first blinding flash, it will be darkness and not light (Amos 5.18); the touch of God's judgment will indeed melt the earth (Amos 9.5, RSV). The story of Noah speaks in primordial terms of the return to chaos: the rebuilding is made possible by the grace of God and the faith-response of a few. Change of direction is a matter of life and death. Repentance and judgment are magnetic poles which govern the direction of our *praxis*.

4. *Conscientization and the gospel.* Somewhere at home I have a UNESCO prize award, dated 1949, with this endorsement: 'It is in the minds of men that the defences of peace must be reconstructed'. Such mental and indeed spiritual self-awareness comes, as Paulo Freire has shown, only when people begin to understand who they are, how they came to be in their present predicament, what the nature of their oppression is, and where-in the way to liberation lies. The preservation of the *status quo* depends on the tacit consent of the silent, propagandized and programmed majority. De-stabilization in the interests of *shalom* will occur only as more and more people come to an awareness of what is happening to – what is being perpetrated on – us in our global environment and articulate the eager longing of

creation for true *shalom* (cf Rom 8.19). Such conscientization can be viewed theologically as an expression of the working of the Spirit of truth (John 16.13). It is also a response to the gospel of Christ, whether explicitly or implicitly. For the *shalom* Christ offers is wholeness for the alienated world, the object of God's love: and that wholeness embraces life, community, breaking bread and celebrating the inter-dependence of the one body. Here is a cameo of the new heaven and the new earth, made possible by the groaning and travail of the Cross. And the broken but glorious Christ is one with all who share in spirit the birth-pangs of the new age: giving life for death, hope for despair, inter-dependence for enmity. To point to this new age – its possibilities and its cost – is the vocation of any church that bears the name of the broken Christ. As the Johannine Christ says:

'*Shalom* is my parting gift to you, my own *shalom*, such as the world cannot give. Set your troubled hearts at rest, and banish your fears' (John 14.27, NEB, adapted).

5

The Challenge of Church Decline

Robin Gill

Church decline in Britain today challenges Christians in a number of crucial ways. The first challenge is to recognize that most churches are indeed declining. The second is a sociological challenge, namely to sift patiently through the evidence in an attempt to find out why churches are declining. And the third is to challenge the churches themselves to make the painful changes that may well be necessary if they are to reverse this decline.

It may seem odd to suggest that churches need to be challenged to recognize their current decline. Yet my experience of directing the Church Decline Research Project at Newcastle University suggests that there is still considerable resistance to the notion of church decline. Several reactions have become apparent. One is to regard church decline as a very temporary phenomenon. Slight rises in membership or ordination statistics in the Church of England or the Church of Scotland soon foster the hope that this decline has begun to reverse. Another is to point to the apparent rapid growth of the House Church Movement or to the resilience of certain evangelical, urban congregations. Those who adopt this approach frequently argue that church decline is only a feature of those sections of the churches which have in effect lost their faith. A quite different – but frequently encountered – response is to argue that churches are not about numbers at all. Their strength or weakness has nothing to do with membership or attendance figures.

Since these reactions are so widespread it is worth unpacking them further. Although each makes some valid points, I am convinced that they are essentially diversions. They allow churches to avoid unpalatable evidence about their current weakness. Understandable as this is, I do not believe that the issue of church decline can be disposed of so easily.

Responses to church decline

The 1987 figures for the Church of England, released in October 1989, might at first suggest that decline is beginning to cease. Numbers on the Electoral Roll are slightly up on those for the previous year and average Sunday attendance has held steady for three years at 2.5% of the English population. Methodists too have begun to express the hope that their conscious policy of addressing church decline is beginning to work. In both churches there is a slight note of optimism. And the first volume of the Bible Society/MARC Europe 1979 census, *Prospects for the Eighties,* argued hopefully that 'the rate of decline in church membership in the late 70s is slower than that in the early 70s' and that 'attendance for most larger Protestant denominations is declining at a slower rate than membership, and is increasing for the smaller denominations. Overall it is slightly increasing' (p. 5).

Unfortunately a more long-term view of the British churches must question this optimism. Indeed, the second volume of *Prospects for the Eighties,* despite attempting to isolate signs of church growth, argued that 'any discussion of church growth must take place in the context of overall church decline. The actual number of practising Christians in England is declining and has been so for most of this century' (p. 7).

The Victorians carried out a number of church censuses, the first a national census uniquely sponsored by the government in 1851 and others carried out locally by newspapers and periodicals from 1881 to 1903. And Victorian clergy in the same period were regularly asked by their bishops to assess average Sunday attendances and the relative strength of other denominations. Most of this evidence is still uncorrelated.[1] Had this been done before it would have been only too obvious that the Church of England at least has been declining in numerical terms since the 1860s.

Average Sunday attendances (even with the ambiguities attached to the term 'average') are by far and away the most important numerical indicators of church vitality. It is small comfort to a church to know that a majority of people require its services for funerals or a still higher proportion for weddings and baptisms. Even festivals, encouraging as they might be to congregations at the time, can provide a stark contrast to the regular worship of churches. Small congregations meeting week by week in large buildings are only too conscious of church decline.

Diminishing congregations and a steady decline in relation to the overall population do seem to have characterized both urban and rural churches in most denominations. However, it is decline in the Church of England that can be demonstrated most fully.[2] In the 1851 Religious Census, aggregated morning and evening attendances in London amounted to 17.7% of the total population: by 1887 this had declined to 13.6%: and by 1903 to 9.6%. These are census figures: they cover all the churches in London. A sample survey for 1928 suggested that churchgoing had already declined to 4.8% and one for 1962 to 3.7%. Bible Society/MARC Europe census figures for average weekly attendance for 1975 suggest that it was down to 2.8% and for 1979 to 2.5%. The Church of England's own statistics for 1985 for the two London dioceses suggest a further drop in average Sunday attendance to 1.7%. Even though the criteria differ somewhat from census to census, the overall pattern of systematic decline is clear. Further, this pattern is corroborated by the London clergy returns to their bishop between 1842 and 1900, now held in the Lambeth Palace Library.

The Free Churches fared scarcely better. They expanded vigorously in many urban and rural areas between the 1850s and the 1880s. They even increased, or at least maintained, their share of urban churchgoers in some areas (contrary to the theory that it is urbanization as such which leads to church decline — clearly not the urban churches' experience in the United States either). In London, the Free Churches' morning and evening aggregated attendances amounted to 13.3% in 1851 and to 13.1% in 1887. Since only the first unambiguously included Sunday School attendances, this may actually represent a slight improvement. Ironically, though, individual churches were on average emptier. Churches which were two-thirds full in the morning in 1851 were just one-third full in 1887. In other words, the Free Churches had expanded buildings faster than congregations. But by 1903 attendances had also dropped, to 10.7%, by 1918 to 4.9%, and by 1975 to 3.5%, reaching only

3.6% by 1979. More detailed studies of individual Free Churches suggest that Wesleyan Methodists were the first to decline in London, mirroring the Church of England's decline quite closely. By 1903 even the recently vibrant Salvation Army was recording significantly reduced congregations.

Set against these massive, long-term declines, small rises in membership today must appear relatively insignificant. And it is even possible that apparent signs of change – such as the vitality of a number of urban, evangelical churches – actually disguises or even exacerbates church decline. An analysis of recent diocesan returns suggests that if these churches are removed from the statistics, then average Sunday attendances elsewhere are still declining. It is even possible that by drawing members from surrounding parishes, such 'successful' churches actually serve to weaken their neighbours. The net result is more empty churches overall. Even the apparent 'success' of the House Church Movement may have a similar effect, although as yet information is still too thin about the previous church attachments of its members.

But what of the objection to the effect that statistics are irrelevant to church decline? Churches are not numbers but communities. Their strength or weakness cannot be assessed in numerical terms, since it is perfectly possible to have numerically strong but spiritually weak churches, and *vice versa*.

I have much sympathy with this perspective. It would be theologically disastrous to equate churches with the crude numbers of churchgoers. And the Kingdom of God is certainly not to be equated with institutional churches. Elsewhere I have criticized some of the more egregious parts of Church Growth literature for coming near to making such equations and for identifying 'success' with 'numbers'.[3] Instead I have argued that it is corporate worship, rather than crude numbers, which is at the centre of my ecclesiology and it is its demise over the last hundred years that concerns me so deeply.

What I have argued[4] is that in corporate worship we express and deepen our relationship to God. Theistic claims and language are by their nature elusive. They cannot be codified or captured any more than can the claims and terms of the artist, the musician, the poet or the lover. Although all can be depicted and analysed in cognitive terms, those who engage seriously in them know that such terms are partial and ultimately inaccurate. There is no substitute for art, music, poetry or love – they can be known in depth only by those who immerse themselves within them. Similarly, I believe that it is only within corporate worship that we can really make sense of Christian signs and symbols. Within corporate worship belief becomes commitment, words become the Word, actions become sacraments, singing becomes hymnody, and hopes become prayers.

Given this theological commitment it may be hardly surprising that I believe that the slow demise of churchgoing in Britain should be a matter of deep concern for Christians. Without falling into the trap of maintaining that large-scale churchgoing is *necessarily* a sign of the Kingdom, it is surely not encouraging that so few people today actively participate in corporate worship. If the latter really is the lifeblood of Christian faith, then its demise must augur badly for the dissemination of this faith. Of course the quality of worship is still vital, and this can be sustained without a great quantity of churchgoers. And of course outreach and social action must also be included in an adequate ecclesiology. Yet, having agreed to all of that, numerical church decline remains as a challenge to Christians in Britain today.

It is also a challenge to sociologists. One of the many paradoxes of the sociology of religion as it has developed over the last twenty years is that it has given more attention to sects of new religious movements than it has to long-established denominations or churches. With important exceptions[5] the latter have not received the sort of detailed attention that one might expect given their prevalence and size. In part this may be due to lingering suspicions of 'Religious Sociology' and to the ecclesiastical control often thought to lurk behind it in France. It may also be due to the sheer difficulty of analysing amorphous religious institutions. Small-scale religious bodies are more sociologically controllable at both levels. Whatever the reason, long-established churches remain relatively unresearched.

Even when sociologists have shown an interest in churches they have typically relied upon generalized data. *Churches and Churchgoers*,[6] invaluable as it is as a source of historical information about national church membership, is notoriously lacking in information about Sunday-by-Sunday churchgoing as such and tends to put forward variables related to general church decline in a highly impressionistic manner. And the now vast literature on secularization frequently avoids statistical data altogether: or else it uses *both* statistics related to church decline in Europe and statistics showing persisting (but supposedly epiphenomenal) churchgoing in the States as indications of secularization.[7]

In contrast, a number of younger social historians have shown a developing interest in churches as social phenomena. Stephen Yeo's detailed study of Reading in the nineteenth and early twentieth centuries is already well known to sociologists of religion.[8] Rather less well known is Jeffrey Cox's *The English Churches in a Secular Society: Lambeth, 1870–1930*,[9] James Obelkevich's *Religion and Rural Society: South Lindsey 1825–1875*,[10] and Callum Brown's *The Social History of Religion in Scotland Since 1730*.[11] Together they suggest that there is considerably more data available on churches as social phenomena than is often imagined and that this data is directly relevant to understanding the decline of most British churches throughout the twentieth century. Far from being generalized studies, they each show that an intense analysis of churches in a confined area (even Brown's study is highly concentrated upon Glasgow and parts of the Borders) yields insights that cannot be deduced from national church membership statistics.

What emerges from this, I believe, is the realization that such intense study of churches at a local level is a prerequisite for understanding the social factors that affect them. This in itself would be a standard premise in the sociological study of sects or new religious movements. Ever since the 1950s, and in particular Bryan Wilson's pioneering *Sects and Society*,[12] the detailed local study of small-scale religious bodies has been preferred to generalized discussions of them as national, or international, institutions. Presumably this is based upon the realization that national information is often gathered selectively and on the basis of varying criteria and may not accurately represent the way a body functions in practice.

But this applies *a fortiori* to churches. The claims that a church makes at a national level may or may not be based upon the way it functions in practice at the local level. Indeed, part of the skill of the social scientist involves comparing claims with actual behaviour. To make such comparisons there is no substitute for detailed empirical research and it has, perhaps, been the most signal failing of the literature on secularization that it has seldom been based upon such research.

It is on these premises that my own research over five years on church decline is based. It focusses specifically on the North East of England (principally Northumberland) and is an attempt to produce an empirical map of churches there which isolates the factors responsible for their decline. I believe that it is only on such a basis that an effective challenge can be made to the churches to change. This chapter is written after a year of this research and offers an indication of the directions that it has already taken and, more briefly, may take over the remaining four years.

Church decline in rural Northumberland

The pilot study for my research[13] has involved an extended analysis of fourteen adjacent parishes in North Northumberland. Together they represent one of the most deeply rural parts of England, with the Scottish Border to their north and west, and contain no town much larger than 2,000 people at any point since 1801. They stop well short of Alnwick to the south and Berwick-upon-Tweed and the Coast to the east. In 1801 the total population of this area was 13,971, at its height in 1851 it was 17,557, and today it is just 7,070: there has been continuous depopulation since 1851. It thus offers the sociologist a highly rural comparitor for the intensely urban areas that characterize the south of the county.

This was an area which experienced considerable Border warfare up to the seventeenth century (most notably Flodden Field in 1513), but which has subsequently been rich farming land. To study the physical presence of churches in it I divided history since the restoration of the monarchy (when church records became more available) into four arbitrary but equal periods of time: 1661–1740; 1741–1820; 1821–1900; 1901–1980.

In the first period the Church of England was particularly active. In nine of the fourteen parishes an incumbent became resident and a new vicarage was built for him. One church was enlarged and nine others were renovated. In addition seven Dissenting (using the term technically simply to denote non-established denominations) chapels/churches were built, one was enlarged and four manses were built.

In the second period, nine Church of England churches were renovated, five enlarged and one further parish received a resident incumbent, with a vicarage built for him. In addition, four Dissenting churches were built, four were enlarged, and six new manses were built.

The third period was the busiest of all. In it all but one of the fourteen Church of England parishes renovated their parish church, all but two built new vicarages, seven additional chapels or mission halls were built, and all the parishes now had their own resident incumbent (three of which had total populations of less than 300 and, in the case of one of these, of less than 200). Further, fifteen new Dissenting churches were built, three were enlarged, six were renovated, and seven new manses were built. Yet ironically this period experienced continuous depopulation from 1851.

This depopulation characterized the whole of the fourth period. No new churches were built or enlarged, although seven Church of England churches were renovated, three vicarages were built and three Dissenting churches were renovated. However, uniquely in this period, in eight Church of England parishes the incumbents ceased to be resident and their vicarages were sold, four mission halls were sold, and thirteen Dissenting churches and eleven manses were sold.

Using the returns from the 1851 Religious Census it would appear that altogether the churches and chapels in the area had 11,034 seats, sufficient for 63% of the total population (and, in reality far more, since some of the parishioners would have been quite small!). Yet, despite continuous depopulation churches continued to be built right up to the end of the nineteenth century. By 1901 there would (on the basis of the 1851 Religious Census and subsequent local estimates for additional or enlarged church buildings) have been 13,049 seats for a total population of only 10,970. Of these seats the Dissenters had 8,704 and the Church of England 4,345. Further, an excess of church seating capacity over total population characterized this area from the 1890s until the 1970s.

Unless there was a dramatic rise in churchgoing between 1851 and 1901, churches which were only 49.3% occupied at the main service on Mothering Sunday in 1851 must have been considerably emptier (despite folk memories) by 1901. If the churchgoing rate had stayed steady, the dual effects of depopulation and increased church seating would have resulted in only 22.1% of these seats being occupied at the main service on a comparable Sunday in 1901. If the churchgoing rate had declined the situation would clearly have been considerably worse. Even if there had been a dramatic increase it would have had to have reached 58% of the total population for churches to have appeared as full (but no more) as they were in 1851.

A detailed study of Clergy Returns to the Bishop of Durham in 1866, 1874 and 1878, and to the Bishop of Newcastle in 1887, suggests that average attendances in the Church of England reached their peak in 1866 and declined thereafter. The 1851 Religious Census asked incumbents to estimate actual attendances on Mothering Sunday and average adult church attendances. If the latter are used, aggregated average attendances for the area were 2,342 in 1851 (13.3% of the total population), 2,884 in 1866 (17.6% pop.), 2,237 in 1874 (15.0% pop.), 2,437 in 1878 (16.3% pop.) and 2,039 in 1887 (15.0% pop.) Further, attendances at the main service at the three largest churches in the area were in 1887 estimated to be only half those of 1851. In other words, less actual attendances were spread over more church buildings.

A very similar pattern emerges from the detailed study of Presbyterian Communion Rolls and attendances (where available), average attendances at Mass at the three Catholic churches in the area, and membership records of the five small Primitive Methodist chapels. Each showed a pattern of expansion, followed by a slow reduction of attendance/membership, concluding with the closure of church buildings and the loss of a resident minister/priest. Perhaps surprisingly, Catholics contracted first: their combined Easter Mass attendances were 234 in 1849, 480 in 1855, but had declined to 297 in 1861, to 187 in 1892 and to just 109 in 1899. Presbyterian churches characteristically reached a peak of Communion Roll membership in the 1860s or 1870s, and then declined rapidly, closing their first major church (seating over 1000) in 1903. The Primitive Methodists had a much smaller membership, which expanded later, reaching a highpoint of 260 in 1888, but reducing to 160 by 1908 and closing all but two of its chapels by the 1980s.

Real, and not just perceived, decline in attendances has now characterized all of the churches in the area. A census that I conducted of the remaining 29 churches of all denominations (out of 45 in 1901) at Pentecost 1988 suggested that there were 636 attendances of all ages (9.0% pop.). On Mothering Sunday in 1851 there were estimated to be 5,436 attendances at morning services (31.0% pop.: afternoon/evening services represented just 7.9%).

From a detailed analysis of these declining rural churches it has been possible to isolate three factors which directly relate to this phenomenon of over-capacity in the context of ongoing depopulation and which can be identified as causal factors in church decline.

The first of these is the actual closing of churches. Each of the four denominations has closed churches. The Presbyterians, who constituted three-quarters of churchgoers in the area in 1851, but now less than half, have closed the most. By examining those Communion Rolls which also record individual attendances it is possible to map out the way individuals respond to a church closure. Characteristically, membership and attendance diminish rapidly as closure nears, only half of the remaining members actually transfer to a neighbouring church after closure and then are sigificantly less regular in their attendance at the new church than they were at the old.

The second factor involves a change in relationship between ministers and congregations. If in 1851 there was one church per minister, in the 1980s there are three churches per minister (across denominations). The ratio of population to minister has changed rather less: in 1851 there were 605 people per minister, in the 1980s there are 707 per minister. However, multiple charges now characterize all denominations (although the Catholics are currently reducing their three churches by at least one). Leslie Francis' empirical research suggests that ministers with three or more churches become significantly less effective and their congregations reduce accordingly.[14]

The third factor is small, and increasingly elderly, congregations in large, empty church buildings. In one church, which seats some 500, there is now a congregation of five. And none of the other churches were remotely full at Pentecost 1988. It is not difficult to see that it is today more difficult for the marginal churchgoers to attend church (without feeling too conspicuous) than it was in 1851. A measure of this change is the changed ratio between Easter communions and average attendances on other Sundays. In the Church of England quarterly communions represented just 2.1% of the total population in 1810–14, 2.2% in 1857, 1.8% in 1887, but in 1986 Easter communions represented 9.4%. But in 1986 this was over twice estimated average attendances (3.6% pop.), whereas in the 1850s it represented just 17% of aggregated average attendances. Similarly amongst Presbyterians today, quarterly communions represent at least double average congregations, whereas in the 1850s they were slightly less than aggregated average attendances. In both instances it may be the less committed church members (i.e. the non-communicants) who are now largely absent from public worship.

The effects of church rivalries

The next stage of my research involved asking two questions. First, why did churches continue to build in the face of de-population and their own evident decline? Second, did this phenomenon of overcapacity – leading to church closures, shared ministers, and sparse, elderly congregations – happen elsewhere in rural Britain.

To answer the first question I examined in detail in *Competing Convictions* the written records left by the four denominations. What emerged is a very considerable degree of inter-church rivalry. The Bishop of Durham's questions in 1810 and 1814 to his clergy show that he was as concerned about the presence of 'Papists' as of Dissenters: 'Are there any reputed Papists in your Parish or Chapelry? How many, and of what Rank? Have any persons been lately perverted to Popery?'[15] The clergy responses from North Northumberland show instead that they were predominantly concerned about the Presbyterians. By 1861 the Bishop of Durham dropped all reference to 'Papists', but not questions about Dissenters. In response one incumbent wrote, in terms similar to those of others: 'The special hindrance to ministerial success in all the Border Parishes is the lamentable extent of Presbyterian Dissent.' Indeed, throughout the second half of the nineteenth century the Church of England continued to write about the 'threat' of Presbyterianism. So, in 1891, the Bishop of Newcastle asked: 'What are the chief hindrances to the success of your Pastoral labours?' One incumbent responded bluntly: 'The struggle of Dissenters to keep their Ministers: dislike to Forms of Prayer: jealousy of Church: deep prejudice: neglect in the past.'

Ironically, Presbyterians in the area very seldom referred to 'Episcopalians' as they termed them. Instead their rivalries were chiefly with each other. Schisms within particular congregations went back at least to the eighteenth century. However the Scottish Disruption of 1843 created enormous tension amongst local congregations, resulting in several new and rival churches being built in the decade following 1848. Normally prosaic Session minutes became quite animated and, in one case, physical violence erupted within a congregation.

Catholic records in turn suggest that those in authority believed that they were bringing salvation to the area for the first time since the Dissolution. Records assiduously counted 'converts' and churches were described as 'missions'. In an area which already had very evident inter-church rivalries, Catholics and then Primitive Methodists brought more. The strength of these rivalries does seem to explain why they all continued to build in a context of depopulation, even when their own relative decline must have become first apparent. Indeed, the 'mission halls' built by Anglicans in the 1890s were specifically designed to counter decline, in the belief that people did not come to church because the parish church was too far from the people. In reality they must have drawn away even more people from parish churches which were already experiencing real decline.

But did this happen elsewhere? To answer this question I have been examining the seating capacity of the churches for each Registration District in England and Wales given in the 1851 Religious Census against the population figures for the same Districts for 1901. Rather surprisingly this simple exercise reveals that in 84 Registration Districts (out of 623) the seating capacity of the churches in existence in 1851 would have exceeded the 1901 population. Such was the extent of rural depopulation in England and Wales (even allowing for extensive boundary changes between Districts) in the second half of the nineteenth century. In no less than 178 Districts there would have been room in 1901 for over 80% of the population. So, without allowing for any extra church building in rural areas after 1851 (despite abundant evidence that such building did take place), there would already have been a very considerable problem of over-capacity by the end of the century.

Obelkevich's study of South Lindsey misses this crucial point. He sets out very usefully the rivalries between Methodists and Anglicans in the area and the degree to which both built in context of depopulation. Yet he finally puzzles about why churches there were in decline by 1870. Had he examined the seating of the churches in the 1851 Religious Census against the 1901 population for Horncastle, Spilsby and Louth, he might have discovered. In 1851 there was already seating capacity in all of the churches there for 89.9% of the total population. The Church of England alone could have accommodated 43.1% of the population (its average nationally was 29.7%). But by 1901, without any additional churches, the Church of England could have accommodated 52.0% of the population and all the church together 108.4% of the same population. In such circumstances church closures, shared ministers and persisting sparse congregations seem inescapable.

Most remarkably of all, the adjacent Registration Districts of Leyburn, Askrigg and Reeth in North Riding, already had seating capacity for their 1851 population of 105.7%. By 1901 the same churches could have accommodated 172.8% of the population and by 1971 no less than 225.1% of the population. Not surprisingly in 1851, although 30.2% of the population were at the main service on Mothering Sunday, they occupied just 28.5% of available church seating. By 1901 the same churchgoing rate would have filled only 17.5% of available seating.

The 1851 Religious Census also supplies abundant evidence of inter-church rivalry. In every Registration District throughout England and Wales several rival denominations were present. In Askrigg, out of 33 church buildings only 6 belonged to the Church of England: the Independents (Congregationalists) had 9, the Wesleyan Methodists 8, and the Primitive Methodists 3. And so throughout the country. Indeed the rate of church building was accelerating (only in part due to the challenge of urbanization): between 1801 and 1811 1224 new churches were built; another 2,002 were built by 1821; 3,141 by 1831; 4,866 by 1841; and 5,594 by 1851.

Taken together this research suggests that rural churches had a massive problem by 1901, from which they are still trying to recover. Overcapacity, a product of inter-church rivalry in a context of rural depopulation, appears widespread. For those churches which lacked a substantial rural subsidy (i.e. the non-Anglican churches) it has proved disastrous. The closure of Dissenting churches must have characterized much of rural England and Wales throughout the twentieth century. Even the Church of England has been forced to combine livings and in effect return to the clerical pluralism of the eighteenth century.

Future directions for research

The next stage of my research will examine churches in relation to population changes in Newcastle upon Tyne. Naturally the population shifts there were quite opposite (although extensive depopulation did characterize the centre of London during the second half of the nineteenth century). It will be just as important to examine each of the denominations in detail as they sought to respond to massive rural immigration. They clearly did not react in identical manners. For example, Catholics in Newcastle currently have about twice as many average attendances as Anglicans, yet the latter have four times as many church buildings. Further, there are indications from clergy returns to their bishop that a number of the older, city-centre Anglican churches were already struggling by the 1870s, even though general levels of Anglican churchgoing may have declined only slightly up to the 1880s.

Once this stage of the research is complete the next will be to produce a total map of the churches in Northumberland, looking for variations between rural, urban and suburban areas over the nineteenth and twentieth centuries. A sufficiently large data base should allow for these comparisons to be made across denominations. Again the stress will be upon statistical data, although clearly other forms of data must also be taken into consideration (as I have already indicated). Eventually it must also include more elusive groups, such as the House Church Movement. Another aspect which will require attention is the involvement of the churches in the wider community, the study of which Yeo and Cox have done much to pioneer.

Only from careful and meticulous analysis can results be finally expected and, perhaps more importantly, can an effective challenge to the churches be mounted. The comparative data should eventually be able to supply a map of the institutional churches in the North East of England which can generate insights for churches elsewhere in Britain. Indeed, it has already become clear that data about urban churchgoing in London can act as a useful comparitor to urban churchgoing in Newcastle. Vigorously competing denominations, new churches being built even when existing churches were less than half full, and subsequent widespread church closures, seem to have characterized both urban areas.

This research is already beginning to suggest that over-building characterized both rural and urban churches in the late nineteenth century. Most denominations, with the instructive exception of the Roman Catholic Church, have inherited the legacy of this problem throughout the twentieth century. For some it has been more obvious than others. Both the English Methodists (especially after the Union) and the Church of Scotland have been aware of this legacy and have closed many buildings. The Church of England, in contrast, has closed churches only reluctantly and continues to subsidize many parishes which would not otherwise be viable. But denominations have yet to act together to assess their own needs, and the needs of the people they seek to serve, ecumenically.

Just as importantly, even in remote rural areas and in largely unchurched urban priority areas they have for the most part continued to provide separate clerical 'cover'. Even when a minister looks after a very extensive, but sparsely populated, area, few denominations have planned effective ecumenical co-operation. And there has as yet been little sustained, rigorous testing of new forms of non-stipendiary clerical and lay ministry. Doubtless the physical defects of the churches will not account for the whole of twentieth-century church decline. It would be absurd to imagine that they might. Yet I am increasingly convinced by this ongoing research that they do hold important clues. They may also suggest important remedies which churches could actually do something about – if they have the will.

III

The Practice of the Church and the Practice of Ministry

6

Lex Orandi Lex Credendi

Duncan B. Forrester

At the heart of Christian practice there stands worship – the strange, distinctive and characteristic activity of the people of God. In worship God is glorified and enjoyed, the mystery of his purposes is glimpsed, however faintly, and God's people are united with their Lord and nourished for life in God's service. There is, of course, an awesome provisionality and incompleteness in our practice of worship: all earthly worship is necessarily partial and imperfect, a looking forward and anticipation of the joyful and glorious praise of heaven, where worship finds its fulfilment and perfection. But it is also true that God can and does use for his glory and the good of humankind our frail and stumbling efforts to worship God.

To affirm the centrality of worship within Christian practice is to suggest not only that worship is an indispensable component of Christian practice, but that it is the centre without which all else falls apart, the point from which one may extrapolate the other dimensions of Christian practice, the part that sustains and clarifies all the rest. Such an affirmation would not be universally acceptable. For example, the liberation theologian José P. Miranda in his *Marx and the Bible*[1] argues that in the Bible there is a consistent teaching that doing justice is the only true service of God, and the cult is regarded either as an irrelevance, or as a cloak for oppression. Miranda overstates his case. But it *is* true that in both testaments there is plentiful criticism of worship when it becomes a substitute for doing justice, or worship which has become separated from life and ethics, an autonomous self-contaned sphere, as it were. And this reminds us of the truth that worship segregated from the rest of life in fact becomes false worship. True worship must infect and reflect the whole of practice, as it is an offering of the wholeness of life to God, and recognizes God's concern with every aspect of worldly existence.

A second group of people who would challenge our statement about the centrality of worship are those who so stress the importance of preaching that worship becomes little more than the preliminaries to the sermon, or the setting for the proclamation of the Word. This generates an extremely didactic understanding of worship. It is to do with words and ideas rather than activity. The people become recipients, 'hearers' (to use the old Scots term for churchgoers), essentially passive. But although this view fails to retain a proper balance and complementarity between word and sacrament and impoverishes the practice of worship, it also reminds us that the Word must have a crucial place in Christian worship, and that worship is not only our activity but the place where God has graciously promised to be present with his people to nourish, encourage and teach them.

In a memorable passage Michael Polanyi, scientist, philosopher and seminal Christian thinker, says this of Christian worship:

> It resembles not the dwelling within a great theory of which we enjoy the complete understanding, nor an immersion in the pattern of a musical masterpiece, but the heuristic upsurge which strives to break through the accepted frameworks of thought, guided by intimations of discoveries still beyond our horizons. Christian worship sustains, as it were, an eternal, never to be consummated hunch; a heuristic vision which is accepted for the sake of its irresolvable tension. It is like an obsession with a problem known to be insoluble, which yet follows against reason, unswervingly, the heuristic command, 'Look at the Unknown!' Christianity sedulously fosters, and in a sense permanently satisfies man's craving for mental dissatisfaction by offering him the comfort of a crucified God.[2]

Worship stimulates, provokes and encourages enquiry; it points towards the truth and sustains seekers of truth; but it only indicates in paradoxical and fragmentary ways the nature of the truth which 'we see in a mirror dimly' until at the last we encounter the truth 'face to face' (I Cor.13.12). Polanyi's concern is with the relation between worship and enquiry in general, but he believes in a close organic relationsip between theology and other sciences: all are nourished, kept to their task, and pointed steadily towards the truth by worship. Our concern in this chapter is the exploration of the relation of worship and theology, the ways in which worship guides theology and points towards its content, and the ways in which theology may purify, enrich and shape worship. We have here a kind of case study in the relation of theology and practice, and an issue which has attracted interest and controversy down the ages.

We will not here go into the origins or the complicated history of the epigram *lex orandi lex credendi*, law of praying, law of believing.[3] 'The old saying', wrote Karl Barth, 'Lex orandi lex credendi, far from being a pious statement, is one of the most profound descriptions of the theological method'.[4] Yet, for all that, it has been used in a bewildering variety of ways and is capable of numerous and often conflicting interpretations.

First, let us explore some of the possibilities which flow from understanding the adage as saying that the law of prayer, or how we worship, is normative for how and what we ought to believe – more or less the position Polanyi was proposing. This suggests that in some sense worship and prayer are sources of theological truth; or perhaps that theology is explication of what we do and say in worship, reflection on worship and the God we encounter in worship. It would follow that in cases where there is a clear discrepancy between what is done and said in worship and what is believed and taught in theology, it is theology which is to be brought into line with worship. 'Tell me how you pray,' runs the proverb, 'and I will tell you how you *ought* to believe.' Worship here provides a source, data and norms for doing theology; and it becomes easy to regard theology as quite simply an aspect or dimension of worship. Theology is not simply prayerful discussion or meditative reflection in the presence of God, but itself *doxology*, the praise of God. In their different ways the meditations of St Anselm and the hymns of Charles Wesley are splendid examples of theology as worship, and worship as theology.

This approach is exemplified in much of the early history of dogma.[5] Orthodox christology and the doctrine of the Trinity, for instance, cannot simply be read off scriptural texts. What we know of the earliest Christian worship suggest that this generated questions to which doctrinal formulation attempted to provide answers and interpretations. The New Testament, for example, offers abundant evidence that the worship of the church involved ascribing divine titles, particularly *kyrios*, to Jesus from the earliest times. We might note, for instance, the use of the Aramaic *maranatha* ('Come, Lord'), a liturgical prayer addressed to Jesus, in I Cor.16, 22, together with passages such as Phil.2.10–11: 'That at the name of Jesus every knee should bow, in heaven and on earth and under the earth, and every tongue confess that Jesus Christ is Lord to the glory of God the Father.' Extracanonical evidence suggests that in the early church worship was offered to Jesus as divine, even if official liturgies, when they began to appear, preferred that prayer should be offered to the Father *through* the Son. But this did not, of course, imply any questioning of the divinity of the Son, or of the appropriateness of offering him divine honours. Indeed one of the commonest objections to the Arians was that they worshipped a Jesus whom they believed to be a creature, less than divine. A major motive for christological formulation was therefore explaining and legitimating how Christians could be monotheists and yet offer divine honours to Jesus; christology arises as a necessary explanation of how Christians worship. The experience of worship demands theological explication.

The development of the doctrine of the Spirit follows not dissimilar lines. The fact that baptism was in the three-fold name was used by Athanasius, Basil and other Fathers as evidence for the divinity of the Spirit as a distinct *hypostasis*, a dogma which it was widely recognized could hardly be established from scripture alone. And as a consequence we must recognize that the doctrine of the Trinity has its tap-root in Christian worship: only thus were Christians able to make more or less coherent sense of the varied and often inconclusive evidence of scripture together with their experience of God in the practice of worship. What was said and done in worship was a major factor in the development of doctrine.

Few Protestants would be in any way uneasy about regarding the Lord's Prayer as a model of prayer, and indeed as a source for our understanding of God. It is, after all, in the Bible! Cyprian spoke of it as the *lex orandi*, and the churches of the

Reformation not only use it in their worship but commonly base the teaching on prayer in their catechisms and confessions on the clauses of the Our Father. But matters become more controversial if we talk of articulating the theology implicit in the action of the Lord's Supper, drawing theological and ethical conclusions from what we say and do in the central act of Christian worship. It is important to remember that Christians were breaking bread together in obedience to the Lord long before the accounts of the Last Supper were written down, and that the eucharistic theology in Paul and in John is clearly reflection on Christian worship. Paul shared many times with his fellow believers in the Lord's Supper before he recalled the Corinthian church to the authentic practice which he had received from the Lord and delivered to them (I Cor.11.23). Paul in this passage is explaining, theologizing and correcting a practice which was already in existence. And he is drawing out ethical implications from the practice: the gluttony of the rich and their humiliation of the poor is so radical a denial of the authenticity of the rite that 'it is not the Lord's Supper that you eat' (I Cor.11.20).

Is it then legitimate for us to derive from the action of the Lord's Supper theological and ethical positions which are not to be found explicitly in the New Testament? Consider, for example, this passage by a left-wing British Roman Catholic:

> The liturgy is radically egalitarian in its basic conceptions. And in this sense it is a scandal in the eyes of a world which is dedicated to quite other social structures – a world based on differences of 'intelligence', 'ability', 'attainment', 'class', 'wealth', 'status', 'rank', or even 'race' and 'religion'. Inevitably then the problem of the liturgy is a problem of creating the Christian community in a condition of tension with the world. That is, quite clearly and obviously, a political problem. For it is a question of achieving a radically egalitarian society, with nothing but functional differentiation in it, against the grain of what is experienced elsewhere. This is the basic reason why a genuine understanding of the theology of liturgy must involve, in a general sense, a socialist commitment.[6]

In this passage we find an assumption that the eucharist is a constant manifestation of the true nature of Christian *koinonia* which is sharply at variance with the way the world is structured.

This seems quite unexceptionable. Nor in principle is the effort to extract from the Lord's Supper ethical implications different from what Paul does in First Corinthians 11 and elsewhere, except that Paul seems concerned primarily for the ordering of the inner life of the Christian community while Wicker draws conclusions for the social and political orders and suggests that the eucharist points towards a specific ideological orientation in politics. But unless we think of church and world as two totally separate spheres – and this is certainly not Paul's view – it seems inevitable that efforts are made to spell out the secular social and political commitments that participation in the Lord's Supper involves. The Johannine saying, 'The bread which I shall give *for the life of the world* is my flesh' surely implies that the body broken on the cross and the bread broken and shared among believers are both for the life of the world. To share that bread involves quite specific commitments to the hungry neighbour and to the needs of the world. We would then suggest that it is not only legitimate but necessary to explore the theology and the ethics implicit in what happens in the central and perennial acts of Christian worship.

But does that mean that we can derive new theological insights from the development of Christian worship and devotion? Protestants find this a particularly acute problem in relation to Roman Catholic mariology. Historically it would seem that the cult of Mary in popular devotion developed well in advance of its various stages receiving official endorsement, theological articulation or dogmatic definition. Both Bernard of Clairvaux and Thomas Aquinas, for example, used the fact that the church observed a feast of Mary's nativity as a kind of proof or confirmation of her sanctification before her birth.[7] And in the definitions of the Immaculate Conception (1854) and the Assumption (1950) the widespread and prolonged expression of these beliefs in worship is used as a major argument, although care is taken to suggest, misleadingly, that popular piety was in fact always under the careful control of the *magisterium*.[8]

Protestants traditionally have considerable reserve about this whole mode of theological argumentation, because they see popular piety as a thoroughly ambiguous phenomenon, by no means consistently reflecting the Holy Spirit's leading into all truth. They characteristically resist any suggestion that the development of forms of worship on its own is capable of producing new truths. This suspicion is however perfectly compatible with accepting that the universal and central thrusts, symbols and emphases of Christian worship, have some normative role in theology, helping with the clarification, confirmation and development of doctrine rather than producing new truths. Worship does not create doctrine *ex nihilo.* as it were.

Protestants are coming to recognize that the relation between theology and worship is a more complex and dynamic one than their traditional insistence that theology must control, inform and determine Christian worship might suggest. This is indeed how Protestants have tended to understand the epigram, *lex orandi lex credendi*: the law of believing, or theology, is the law of praying or worship. This, our second interpretation, is of course the contrary of the first, and represents a characteristically, but not exclusively, Protestant view. The Reformation's desired return to the purity and simplicity of the worship of the early church is in one sense, of course, impossible of achievement – the practice of one age and culture cannot be transferred without modification to another. The Reformation did indeed make a notable effort to reform worship, stripping away mediaeval accretion and pious elaborations to make the significance and structure of Christian worship more clear than it had been for many centuries, and attempting to produce patterns of worship which were authentically Christian and free of adulteration of folk piety. There were, it is true, important differences in the approaches adopted by the Lutherans and the Calvinists. Here as elsewhere, the Calvinists were more radical, advocating and carrying through a transformation of worship based on the conviction that only that explicitly commanded in scripture, or for which there was explicit biblical precedent, was to be permitted. The Lutherans were less thoroughgoing, seeing scripture as providing general guidelines, and excluding certain things, but leaving a large area of freedom, so that more could be taken over consciously from the mediaeval tradition than was allowable in Calvinist circles. One instance is the case of hymnody. For long Calvinists insisted that only psalms or scripture paraphrases might be sung in church. Only very gradually – in Scotland hardly before the nineteenth century – were 'hymns of human composition' admitted to public worship. From the beginning, in contrast, the Lutheran churches, like the Wesleyans, fostered a lively, prolific and rich tradition of hymnody, which in modern times has been shared with all the churches of the oikumene. Neither Lutheran nor Calvinist was as successful as they hoped in sloughing off mediaevalism in worship. But for our present purposes the important point is to note how clearly and unambiguously the Reformation affirmed that the Bible and doctrine must control the worship of the church. It was not only important that true doctrine should be preached; it must also be expressed in the approved ways of worship and in particular in the administration of the sacraments.

The tendency of some Protestant churches to give their service books almost the status of confessions of faith is more than an indication that the *lex orandi* is effectively controlled by the *lex credendi*. Here the form and content of worship is not the choice of congregation or clergy, but is authoritatively laid down so that it expresses the official theology. Service books are used to conserve orthodoxy, so that eventually the service book itself comes to be used as a theological *locus*. The same is true in some churches of the hymnal. The situation is more confused in churches which emphatically affirm the need for theological control over worship but have no mandatory liturgy or service book. The result is that theological control exists in name only, and the form and content of worship is left almost entirely to the whim of the minister or the conservatism of the congregation.

It is not without interest to note the multitudinous similarities between what the Reformation did and attempted (for achievement often fell far short of what was desired, in the establishment of weekly communion, for instance) and the impact of the modern liturgical movement. The project of the liturgical movement which now so deeply affects the worship of churches of every tradition gives to the Bible and the primitive church a normative status. But the liturgical movement is not an attempt simply to restore the primitive; nor is it the endeavour to adapt worship to the modern world, marrying liturgy and the Spirit of the Age, as it were. Rather it is the endeavour to renew worship in the light of enlarged and deepened biblical and theological understanding in the conviction that this will also involve a fresh relevance to the needs and issues of the day. The law of believing here is to be the law of worship and of prayer.

We have said enough of the two contrary interpretations of *lex orandi lex credendi*, that worship should shape theology or that theology should control worship, to make it clear that neither is without its serious problems. But that does not mean that we are obliged to dismiss the epigram as valueless. Other, more lively and fruitful relations are possible between theology and worship, theory and practice. The interaction between them may be likened to an ongoing dialectic, or perhaps to a hermeneutic circle. One could well argue that Christian theology must be rooted in worship and should flow into doxology, the giving of praise to God. Suggestions such as that language affirming or presupposing the incarnation and the divinity of Christ is acceptable in worship but is no longer tenable in theology separate worship and doctrine in an intolerable way which would prove destructive of the integrity of each. It is surely a central responsibility of theology to monitor as a loving critic the worship, prayer and preaching of the church. Barth was quite correct in affirming this relationship as necessary if theology is to be Christian. A theology which refuses to accept this responsibility may for a time have significance in the academy, but it has lost its churchly relevance. This does not mean that there can be or ought to be total and constant harmony between worship and theology. Each is an exploration into the ultimate mysteries, and at times they will be out of step with one another. We may rejoice to join 'with angels and archangels and all the company of heaven' in praising God even as we agonize about the problems of whether an angelology is possible and our difficulty in articulating what we mean by heaven. But if we believe that the existence of angels must be stoutly denied and heaven is a fruit of false consciousness then integrity would demand that we attempt to excise the angels and archangels and all such language from our orders of worship. But to move between worship and theology convinced that both are orientations towards the same mysteries is exhilarating and challenging in both areas. It is also true that worship provides some important tests of theological positions – can they be prayed or preached? Do they lead into worship? Do they engage reverently as well as rigorously with mysteries which are to be adored, explored and lived out?

Lex orandi lex credendi affirms very simply and directly the truth that worship and theology must be held together in an ongoing interaction for the good of each. Christian worship is a form of practice which sustains and stimulates and challenges the theological enterprise, and serves as a constant demonstration that the truth of God is to be encountered in life, in praise and in prayer as well as in reflection.

7

Theology and Ordained Ministry

Robin Gill

Both theory and practice of ordained ministry illustrate its plurality and its relationship to specific social structures. Any comprehensive historical survey of theological understandings of ordained ministry from one age to another soon reveals a bewildering variety of options. And any thoroughgoing empirical review of ministry, as it exists today in the various churches, shows its pluriformity. The most obvious fact about ordained ministry is that it has been and remains extraordinarily varied. Indeed it soon becomes clear that this empirical pluriformity and theological pluralism owe much to the changing nature of society; any adequate attempt to understand ordained ministry today must first seek to understand the nature of the society within which it is to operate.

A preparedness to relate different forms of ordained ministry to particular socio-political structures is characteristic of Edward Schillebeeckx's *Ministry: A Case for Change*.[1] He argues that 'in church history it is possible to recognize three views of the priest (which are partly socially conditioned): patristic, feudal or mediaeval, and modern'.[2] In the patristic period Schillebeeckx sees the beginning of what he calls the process of the 'clericalization of the ministry'. He traces the division between clergy and laity that was to be formalized in the mediaeval period back to the Roman concept of 'ordo':

In the Roman empire, *ordo* had the connotation of particular social classes differing in status. The senators formed the 'higher order', into which one would be 'instituted' (*in-ordinari* or *ordinari*). Under the Gracchi, an order of *equites* came into being between the *ordo senatorum* and the *plebs*, or the people (here *ordinari* then means becoming an *eques*); only later was the *plebs* itself also an *ordo*. Thus finally people talked of *ordo et plebs*, i.e. the upper, leading class, and the ordinary people, a terminology which not only introduced influence from the Old Testament but also coloured the difference between clergy and the people (laity): after the time of Constantine the church *ordinatio* or appointment to the 'order of office-bearers' clearly became more attractive because the clergy were seen as a more exalted class in the church in comparison with the more lowly 'believers'. The clericalization of the ministry had begun![3]

So, in contrast to the loose differentiations of function apparent in the New Testament, formal 'orders' began to emerge with the closer relations of the church with the Roman empire. In the mediaeval period this formalization took its most rigid character. Schillebeeckx argues that the Third Lateran Council of 1179 and the Fourth of 1215 were the occasions of a fundamental change, whereby men were ordained without being put forward for ordination by a particular community. The notion of a 'proper living' was now conceived in financial, rather than community, terms: 'The implications are clear: the ordained man simply waits for the place to which his bishop will appoint him as priest! *Ordinatio* remains, in the abstract, the appointment of a Christian as minister in a diocesan area, though his specific placing is still left open. Here the claim of the community, which was originally an essential element of *ordinatio*, disappears.'[4] He argues that two non-theological factors were responsible for his fundamental change – feudalism and legalism – both characteristic of the Middle Ages:

Before that, for Christians the boundary between the 'spirit of Christ' and the 'spirit of the world' lay in their baptism: their sense of being accepted into the elect community of God's *ecclesia*; now, with the massive expansion of the church, this boundary came to lie above all at the point of the 'second baptism', that of monastic life ... At a time when virtually everyone was baptized, the boundary between the 'spirit of Christ' and the 'spirit of the world' came to lie with the clergy.

As a result the priesthood was seen more as 'a personal state of life', a *'status'* than as a service to the community; it was personalized and privatized. In particular the new conceptions of law(*ius*) and thus of jurisdiction, brought about a division between the power of ordination and the power of jurisdiction ... lawyers developed the idea of 'sacred power' (*sacra potestas*), strongly influenced by the context in which they lived. *Potestas* is the stake in the whole of the investiture controversy between *imperium* and *sacerdotium*, emperor and pope, and the sphere of their authority. For the theology of the church, however, the division between the power of ordination and the power of jurisdiction meant the opening of the door to absolute ordinations. For although the ordained man might not be assigned a Christian community (i.e., legally speaking, had no *potestas jurisdictionis*), by virtue of *ordinatio* he had all priestly power in his own person.[5]

Many of the points that Schillebeeckx makes are also made by Bernard Cooke, albeit with more awareness of a Reformed perspective, in his seminal *Ministry to Word and Sacraments*.[6] So he argues that 'the late patristic and mediaeval church tried to clarify the reality of priesthood and ministry by issuing laws to regulate the existence of the ordained. Like all positive legislation, these laws dealt with the external social relationships of those in the clerical state (to one another and to other members of the church); and such laws almost necessarily treated the clergy as a class in society, rather than dealing with ministry as an essentially charismatic function ... The present-day fascination of most bishops with the prescriptions of canon law and their appeal to it as the primary guide for interpreting their own role and that of the priests working with them indicate that the legal way of envisaging the ministerial function is still very influential.'[7]

It is evident from these quotations that neither Schillebeeckx nor Cooke are impartial observers of the history of ordained ministry. Writing as Catholics with differing perspectives, both are concerned to distinguish between more and less adequate forms of ministry. Coole does this by examining ministry under five headings; as formation of community, as ministry to God's word, as service to the people of God, as ministering to God's judgment, and as ministry to the church's sacramentality. Under each heading he attempts, first to distinguish the essential features of the New Testament evidence and then to examine ministry in each of the major historical periods. Schillebeeckx's procedure, although very similar, is more obviously restricted to the needs of present-day Roman Catholicism. In his book the Reformation does not play a central role, whereas 'orders', sacraments, power and community become dominant concerns. Both insist that antiquarianism should not be a principle in shaping ministry, but nevertheless both are considerably influenced by their understandings of New Testament ministry. Further, both use sociological and historical-critical methods to understand past forms of ministry. Indeed, Schillebeeckx insists that, 'it emerges from the historical sketch which I have given that the constant in the church's ministry is always to be found only in spenific, historically changing forms'.[8] He finds this insight important, since it suggests that 'church order is not an end in itself. Like the ministry, it too is at the service of the apostolic communities and may not be made an end in itself, or be absolutized.'[9] Indeed, he believes that it is 'a sociological fact that in changed times there is a danger that the existing church order will become a fixed ideology, above all by reason of the inertia of an established system which is therefore often concerned for self-preservation'.[10] On socio-historical grounds he insists that church order is both essential *and* relative. Both he and Cooke believe that a church without some order is an impossibilty, but he is more insistent than Cooke that all actual orders are relative to specific societies.

Both authors have a tendency to use such critical methods as sociology to expose some of the inadequacies of previous forms or understandings of ministry. So the weaknesses of late mediaeval forms of ministry become obvious once their roots in feudalism and mediaeval legalism become apparent. Similarly, once the link with Roman concepts or *ordo* is made, a hierarchical division between clergy and laity can be seen to be spurious. This type of argument is encountered so frequently in the literature on ministry that it is easy to forget that it rests upon a number of fallacies. The most obvious of these is the generic fallacy: to demonstrate the origins of something is to say nothing about its validity. In addition it ignores the obvious starting point for understanding of ministry, namely, that *all* forms and theories of ministry are socially rooted. More positively, such an approach would suggest that it is actually a merit, not a fault, of ministry that it is always so rooted. A form or understanding of ministry that was not shaped by society would be, by definition, a socially irrelevant ministry.

There is a further difference between this understanding of theology and that implicit in Schillebeeckx and Cooke. Despite all the evidence that they provide about the pluriformity and doctrinal ambiguity of ministry throughout Christian history, both are convinced that there are also points of continuity. This conviction leads them at times into some strange logic. So, for example, both believe that the New Testament link between ministry and the Christian community is a theme in all forms of ministry. It is on this basis that Schillebeeckx clearly dislikes private masses. This is very apparent in the text of his book. There (comparing mediaeval and New Testament understandings of ministry) he argues unambiguously: 'If a man has been personally ordained priest, he has the "power of the eucharist" and can therefore celebrate it on his own. For the early church this was quite simply inconceivable.'[11] But then he adds a footnote: 'I am in no way denying the value of a private mass as deep personal prayer, much less its formative value for the priest who celebrates it; I am simply saying that in terms of the priestly ministry and the church, at the least it is very peripheral. A sacrament is the celebration of a local community (of whom a large number will be present), not of a community "envisaged as being there".'[12] It is perhaps obvious why a Dominican feels obliged to add this footnote, but it does fit ill with the rest of his argument. Similarly, Cooke argues that 'community' is still present even in the ministry of those most involved in the controversies surrounding the Reformation: 'At first glance it would seem that the ordained ministry of the Christian churches had betrayed the basic purpose of their office, the formation and preservation of Christian community, for they were a key influence in keeping Christianity divided. Yet it probably would be more fair to say that their perspective grew more limited. They were interested in fostering the community of the faithful but they no longer identified this community with "the great church".'[13] The force of his quotation depends entirely upon conflating two distinct meanings of the term 'community'. In contrast, my understanding of theology would allow that there may be no distinct continuity in the differing forms and theories of ministry in Christian history. Indeed, the only common factor that they may possess might be their common self-description as 'Christian'. It might be possible to identify a cluster of factors making up this ministry, but no single factor may apply to them all.

There is another, more ruthless, option. It can be argued that even though empirically there is no single factor that is found in all forms of ministry that call themselves Christian, there nonetheless *should* be such a factor. That is, for a form or theory of ministry properly to call itself Christian there should be identifiable criteria. It is one of the ironies of Anglicanism, despite its evident pluriformity and doctrinal ambiguity, not least in the area of ordained ministry, that various versions of this position have proved popular.

So, at the theological level, both R. P. C. Hanson[14] and A. E. Harvey[15] argue that there are principles that can be derived from the New Testament which disallow forms of ministry currently practised in the churches (assistant bishops for Hanson and auxiliary priests for Harvey). Both, of course, work in a thoroughly critical tradition of biblical scholarship and neither believes that current forms of ministry can be derived wholly from the New Testament. Yet both believe that there are biblical criteria which allow one to dismiss extant forms or theories of ministry. From a sociological perspective it seems odd to imagine that a church so complex and so lacking a centralized power authority can be led to accept *any* single criterion as essential to ministry. A similar tendency can be seen amongst some of those seeking structural changes in the Church of England (Fenton Morley in the 1960s[16] and Tiller in the 1980s[17]), an extraordinary optimism that so diffuse a church could actually change so radically and could then conform to a single pattern or understanding of ministry. Notoriously, changes in ministry tend to be made *ad hoc* and their justification made *ex post facto* – as the development of the non-stipendiary ministry shows. Structural changes, even when it is admitted that there are no theological objections (as with the ordination of women), are extremely difficult to effect.

The understanding of theology offered here would suggest a less ambitious, less prescriptive approach to ministry. An awareness that *all* forms and theories of ministry (including those currently popular) are shaped by society would suggest greater caution. Even 'biblical principles', which can never be less than central for Christians, must be interpreted and this interpretation is inevitably socially located. The Bible is not a socially independent arbiter for Christians, but a part of their specific

social context from one age to another. In such an understanding of theology it becomes essential to analyse specific
social contexts and not to assume *a priori* that everything can be
conformed to particular New Testament principles. This is not
to underestimate the importance of such principles, but rather
to see them as a part of the continuing social context of
the churches. Similarly, the accumulative traditions of historic
churches inevitably still control their present-day understanding
of issues such as that of ministry. Even when a tradition is
intellectually rejected it is still a part of the inherited social
milieu of the particular church to which it belongs. Only so can
one adequately understand Schillebeeckx's reluctance finally to
reject private masses.

If this understanding of theology is accepted, it becomes
important first to analyse the social context within which
ministry is to function and then, to decide which amongst the
many and varied resources of Christian ministry are most
appropriate to this context. In this way, ministry is recognized as
socially located, as a product of accumulative Christian resources
(Bible, tradition, etc.) and finally as something that has relevance
to particular societies. It is essentially not a timeless state of
being which can afford to ignore the particularities of passing
cultures.

Fortunately, there are now a number of reliable books
analysing the present-day social context of the British churches.
John Habgood in *Church and Nation in a Secular Age*[18] has studied
most of these and has produced an important and accessible
account which can be used for the present purposes. Basing his
study initially on the most recent sociology of religion in this
area, he concludes that Britain is only partially secular: it is also
religiously plural, with strong continuing elements of folk and
civil religion, and with an undercurrent of Christian values.
Within this context he believes that it is important for
the Church of England in particular – despite its declining
congregations – to remain established and to retain its role
of embedding moral values within society. He is strongly
committed against any sectarian attempt to reduce the social
function of the British churches in the interests of producing a
series of strong sects. Further, he argues that there are some
points in a nation's life, particularly in situations of crisis, when
secular pluralism cannot provide values essential for national
survival. It is in these situations that the need for religiously

derived values can be seen and that the specific role of the British churches becomes apparent.

Habgood's analysis is not without difficulties,[19] but it does offer a clear analysis of the present-day religious situation of Britain and an understanding of the role of British churches. It can perhaps be adopted for the moment as a useful indication of one of the paths that contemporary ministry could take. This might be termed the moral or professional role of ministry in a secular-plural society. However, I also believe (and I doubt if Habgood would disagree) that this role should be supplemented by a cultic role, and that if one role is upheld without the other a very partial view of the churches would emerge. If it is the function of the moral or professional role of ministry to embed Christian values into society, it is the function of the cultic role to build local Christian communities, sometimes in quite secular or religiously plural contexts. If the first function belongs properly to the church, the second belongs rather to the sect. Without the first the British churches would become increasingly irrelevant to society at large and without the second they may lose any significant base within local communities. If the second form of ministry most closely resembles the ministry-in-community apparent in the New Testament, the first is adapted specifically to the requirements of an increasingly complex, yet educated, society.

The cultic role of ministry is the more obvious of the two. A number of sociologists believe that it is in this area that the churches in Britain are currently facing their strongest challenge. Bryan Wilson has for long been an exponent of a thoroughgoing secularization mode, viewing Western society as undergoing a lengthy and ineluctable process of religious decline. In his most recent writings, notably in *Religion in Sociological Perspective*,[20] he argues that one of the factors strongly effecting secularization is the decline of local, face-to-face communities in society. He believes that 'religion may be said to have its source in, and to draw its strength from the community, the local, persisting relationships of the relatively stable group ... In essentials, religion functions for individuals and communities, at its worst for a client, and at its best for a fellowship.'[21] But the problem it faces in the West today is that community relationships are increasingly giving way to impersonal, rational, bureaucratic relationships. So, 'the course of social development that has come, in recent times, to make the society, and not the community, the primary locus of the individual's life has shorn religion of its erstwhile function in the maintenance of social order and as a source of social knowledge. Of course, religion does not disappear: institutions survive, consciousness lingers, religious individuals and groups persist. New movements emerge, and often by presenting religion in a more demotic and rationalized form, attract large followings. Yet, whereas religion once entered into the very texture of community life, in modern society it operates only in interstitial places in the system.'[22] This understanding of the social position of religion in the present-day West is very close to that of Peter Berger in *The Heretical Imperative*:[23] (see also Peter L. Berger, Brigitte Berger and Hansfried Kellner, *The Homeless Mind: Modernization and Consciousness*).[24] Wilson is convinced that it is only those sects which have built up strong barriers against the outside world that will be able to survive in an increasingly secular society.

It is not necessary to accept the whole of Wilson and Berger's (rather sweeping) generalizations about Western society, to see that they do point to real processes. It may be possible to build genuine Christian communities in rural Britain which still have strong roots in the community at large, but in many urban (particularly inner urban) areas the only Christian community which can effectively be built is a community which is conscious of standing over and against a largely indifferent and pluralistic society. Within these contexts churches are often faced with the prospect either of ceasing to survive at all or of building a definable community within a society which increasingly lacks community relationships. It is here that the cultic function of ministry does seem to be an appropriate, albeit highly constrained, social response.

However, on its own, this form of ministry, in the setting of an increasingly secular-pluralist society, may tend to push the churches in a more and more sectarian direction. In turn this would mean that they have less and less influence on those outside the churches and that the boundaries between church and society would grow ever more sharply differentiated. If the moral function of the British churches, championed by Habgood, is also to be upheld, it will be necessary to supplement this form of ministry with something else. It is at this point that the relevance of a moral or professional role of ministry can be seen.

Ironically, the 'professional' understanding of ministry has been strongly criticized by a number of recent sociologists. Robert Towler and A. P. M. Coxon in *The Fate of the Anglican Clergy*[25] present a striking challenge to the idea that the ordained ministry is a 'profession' or even an 'occupation'. They argue that the 'professional training' of the clergy fits uneasily alongside other forms of professional training and that there are strong external and internal pressures militating against the clergy having any clear function either in society or in the church. Externally, many of the functions once belonging exclusively to the clergyman are now performed more obviously by a variety of secular professionals. Internally, pastoral and liturgical functions are now shared increasingly by congregations as a whole. Anthony Russell in *The Clerical Profession*[26] has successfully shown that the concept of ordained ministry as 'a profession' is a comparatively recent development. Indeed, it was in the nineteenth century that professionalization took effect, with the Victorians building their clergy large and desirable houses, providing them with good incomes, affording them a distinct place in the social order and requiring them to train in university. He believes that this understanding of the ministry has caused a number of serious deficiencies. So he argues that it has created a form of elitism: 'the clergy's strong attachment to the image of their role as that of a professional man has resulted, in practice, in the restriction of recruitment to that narrow band in the middle and upper midddle class from which the other professions predominantly recruit'.[27] This, in turn, has created a legalistic and almost military church at odds with its voluntary function in modern society. He wishes the churches, instead, to move away from a stipendiary, professional clergy and to stress more the local, unclerical, eucharistic group.

Again, it is not necessary to accept all of these generalizations to find them important and useful. The desire of Towler and Coxon, in particular, to find clear functions which the priest alone possesses may itself be misguided. It is perfectly possible to argue that the only function the priest alone possesses is that of being responsible for *all* the priestly functions being put into effect by the congregation. And it is far from clear from the relevant sociological literature that any of the 'professions' can be seen unambiguously as 'professions'. The clergy are not unique in this respect. Nonetheless, they do point to

some of the difficulties that many clergy experience in a
secular-pluralist society. What neither considers seriously is that
the non-stipendiary ministry actually offers an important new
understanding of the notion of ministry as a profession – or,
more accurately, it heightens a professional feature already
found in some long-standing forms of ministry.

It has become clear that the still-growing non-stipendiary
ministry recruits primarily from certain professional groups,
notably teachers and university lecturers. Despite the hopes of
some of those involved in its inception, it has been less successful
in recruiting working-class candidates. There is a tendency to
regard this as a failure rather than as simply a fact.[28] It is,
though, possible to see it as an important response to a secular-
pluralist society. By-passing the problem of whether or not
ordained ministry is itself a profession, it is increasingly to
be found amongst a wide variety of professions. Thus, non-
stipendiary ministry as it exists in practice represents a form of
priesthood only partially tied to Christian communities, but
which is nonetheless identified as priesthood in secular contexts.
For those in a Reformed tradition this has sometimes appeared
strange: they have argued that it is the job of all Christians to be
Christians in society: it is not a special function of priesthood.
But, from the perspective of a secular-pluralist society, it may
have an important symbolic function. It may also suggest that
stipendiary as well as non-stipendiary (perhaps an increasingly
irrelevant and confused distinction) ministries should see it as
their function to be seen to be involved in society at large. Within
an increasingly educated and 'professional' society, it may
indeed be appropriate that a part of this involvement should
take place actually within professional groupings. Indeed
this type of involvement can avoid some of the dysfunctional
features of clerical professionalism noted by Russell. There will,
of course, sometimes be role conflict in this form of ministry and
it cannot be assumed that Christian values of any sort will
automatically become transposed into these various professions.
There are some professions (notably those in the business,
financial and legal worlds) which present potentially sharp
conflicts for those also attempting to exercise a non-stipendiary
form of ministry. Nonetheless, even in these situations an
important response to a secular-pluralist society may be seen;
Stephen Sykes[29] suggests that conflict itself is not necessarily

uncreative. Such an understanding of theology and ministry might well see this form of ministry as appropriate and significant and as a crucial guard against the British churches being reduced to sects.

8

The Group as Minister

Murray Leishman

Groups of clergy have been meeting with clinical staff in the Royal Edinburgh Psychiatric Hospital on a monthly basis over the last twelve years. I will describe how the Mental Health Forums have developed and set down the central questions they have raised for us about the nature of ministry today. The practical purpose of the Forums is to enable more effective ministry by the churches to people who are psychologically distressed and especially to those who are present, past, or potential National Health Service patients.

We started with the question of the 'minister's visit' to the hospital which is still expected of the minister and priest in Scotland today. Never easy in a general hospital, it can be fraught with difficulty and anxiety im the psychiatric hospital, not only for the visiting minister and the clinical staff, but for the patient. But ministers' visits can also be supportive to the staff and therapeutic to the patient during hospital admission, on return home, and possibly for years more. And since the church represents the only tolerant and friendly human support system available to many patients in their home setting, it is important to give thought, effort and NHS and church time to exploit these visits and to maximize their benefit to the patient in hospital and on recovery. That may mean helping to rehabilitate 'the visit' from being seen as a daunting and dull chore by the minister or an unwelcome intrusion into medical mysteries on the part of some clinicians.

Since most mental patients feel bad and useless inside

themselves, the doctors and nurses who care for them can very easily pick up these same feelings about the work they do on the patient's behalf. An easy way of failing to deal adequately with these feelings is to attribute them to others in the patient's world, such as their family. Clergy are usually associated with family feeling, and individual clergy by their temperament and church culture may be too quick to accept the attribution of uselessness to themselves as if that represented a true state of affairs.

As we quickly discovered in the group, wherever there is care, there is also rivalry. The patient both suffers from this rivalry and will try to exploit it in order to control it as it echoes from his own early life. The best the professional carers can do is to be aware of their rivalry and try to manage it better.

My colleague and I are full-time chaplains in the psychiatric hospital. To launch the clergy work group project we joined forces with a consultant who specializes in community psychiatry.[1] We have been joined intermittently by several other consultants and their trainees as well as by senior nursing staff, social workers and occupational therapists. Each month a process minute of the previous group meeting and an invitation to the next one is circulated to 170 clergy in the hospital catchment area – priests of the Roman Catholic and Scottish Episcopal Churches, ministers of the Church of Scotland, Congregational Union, Baptist Union, Methodist circuit, Salvation Army, Unitarian Church and Faith Mission. The same minutes go to appropriate staff in the Sector Clinical Teams. I act as secretary, chairman and timekeeper for the one-and-a-quarter-hour meetings. Over the twelve-year period as few as two and as many as twenty-two clergy have appeared at group meetings, while clinical staff attendances range from one to five. There are now four meetings per month. Attendances seem to fluctuate in relation to quality of interaction. If people got something last time, they tend to come back for more. The group meetings move through different phases as participation builds up, and as patterns are established, only to change again as new leaders and contributors emerge.

For example, there is what we call the 'tell me doctor' phase, much in evidence at the outset of the project but still recurring. Characteristically, some ministers will try to push the psychiatrists out of the role of colleague – which is what we are trying to establish in the project – into the role of lecturer. Perhaps there will be a call to 'say something about schizophrenia' or 'comment about a newspaper article on alcoholism'. A psychiatrist will duly oblige and describe the incidence of the syndrome, symptoms, diagnosis, treatment programmes and outlook; but there the process tends to stick. An authoritative expert has been found. But, if the psychiatrist responds in a different manner and questions the questioner about *his* experience of dealing with a schizophrenic parishioner or *his* efforts to help a heavy drinker, then something different happens. A living person rather than an 'illness' emerges and the minister has *his* authority confirmed out of his own work experience. The psychiatrist can also select his medical lore more appropriately to fit the profile. The rest of the group often report on the usefulness of such exchanges about the particularities of a case, and may go on to offer parallel experiences and their own reflections on the differences between them. As confidence grows, people are prepared more frankly to ask the group for help with work rather than to propose an abstract topic for discussion.

Example 1: A priest described the family he had just visited at home that day. The son of the house, a young man in his twenties, in a promising professional careeer, without warning to his family, threw himself out of a window and killed himself. There was some indication from his work colleagues that immediately prior to this he had been noticeably depressed. The group entered into a long discussion about the ethics of suicide and the Christian view. As this went on, people in the group seemed to become more and more dejected, the priest dropped out of the discussion at an early stage and became quite preoccupied. This state of affairs was pointed out. At this, the priest revived and said that he had, in fact, been thinking about his struggle to get through to the man's mother. She was a highly educated *grande dame* who alarmed everyone by refusing to show any sign of grief and seemed strangely indifferent to her son's self-destruction. The whole tenor of the discussion changed from that point.

Eventually the priest said, in summing up, that what had happened in the group was similar to what was going on in the family he was caring for. An unreal intellectual discussion had been the group's response. This seemed to him a covering up of people's real feelings of shock and despair about the suicide of a young person and all the feelings that had been stirred up by the account. The intellectual capacity of the young man's family and especially of his mother seemed, in a similar way, to get in the way of any experience of real feeling. The priest had identified, as psychodynamic workers would say, partly with the mother and partly with the young man, but only when the identification came out in the group could he articulate to himself something of what was happening in his pastoral work with the family.

What has been overlooked is the fact of the unconscious as a potent dimension in every aspect of life. Most people are half convinced that symptoms mean something, as Freud demonstrated. Again, people are half convinced that many human difficulties have a root in the life story and especially in the early years. But these two factors on their own do not give a psychodynamic point of view. In addition, the unconscious patterns need to be identified for a truly psychodynamic view to be established. These unconscious things have a remarkable way of getting into every system and popping up at several removes from the agent. This is why, if we are to harness psychodynamic knowledge to pastoral work, it is essential to devise a learning setting where hitheto unrecognized factors may not only be talked about but, from time to time, experienced and then identified in a way that is helpful to the participants in the group. Until there is that element of shared experience, in general and in detail, little progress is made beyond a bookish and half-sceptical preoccupation with Freudian talk. The psychodynamic comment which often followed had the effect of getting the group back to work.

Hard on the heels of the 'tell me doctor' phase in the group meeting and as part of what I take to be the same dependency, will often come angry and aggressive attacks on psychiatrists in general – present company always being excepted! Psychiatrists will be hauled over the coals for 'undermining people's faith' or 'advocating free love as a therapy'. Incidents will be recounted where ministers or priests have felt excluded or humiliated in their hospital work.

At one level, of course, such things do happen. There are rubs and irritations in any inter-professional situation, and when we are anxious and busy we can all be stupid and rude. There was the Olympian young psychiatrist who reduced a senior minister to near-apoplexy by interpreting his interest in a young woman patient in sexual terms. Then there was the colleague who had been asked in haughty tones by a senior psychiatrist 'what he proposed to offer this patient' (his parishioner of long standing) 'which the ward could not supply?' But then, of course, there were the counter-balancing stories about ministers; in the hearing of other staff, one colleague told a very ill patient that 'the sooner he got off these pills and on to his knees the better', or the minister who was reported to have enquired of the anxious parents of a chronically schizophrenic son at the weekly prayer meeting 'have the prayers not healed Jimmy yet?'

It is perhaps useful to have these jarring facts of our rivalry brought out. But the most rewarding work was done when the group went deeper and examined the patient's part in rivalries. Surely it could not be coincidence that we had repeatedly to deal with situations in which the patient had made us into 'the good psychiatrist and the bad minister' or 'the bad psychiatrist and the good minister', much as the child under stress will split his parents. And, of course, when we are given the good parent role we all love to hang on to it – 'this must be true!' – but become irritated when the reverse happens. The great mistake is to underestimate the power of the 'weak' patient to do these things to us, to tickle our vanity, to stir our envy, and to make us feel helpless and frightened. Our professional labels and groupings can look deceptively unassailable. But again this is a large matter which can best be thought of in terms of a particular situation.

Example 2: A minister opened a meeting by saying, rather angrily, that he wished someone would give him a booklist about baby-battering. One or two suggestions were made by a psychiatrist – the social worker was absent that day – and a rather guilty and uneasy general discussion took place about the evils of child abuse. The minister was then asked if he had something specific in mind. At this, he launched into an attack on the local Social Work Department, accusing them of monstrous bungling and described how they allowed a three-year-old child to be fostered by no fewer than five people. He had tried to speak to the senior social workers about the case but had been given the brush-off.

Several ministers in the group worked hard to draw out their colleague by sympathetic questioning, especially about his feelings of humiliation and rage in the face of officialdom.

Apparently, he knew the parents well and they hoped he would get their child back from care. Someone said that 'it must be awful for him to realize he was about to fail them'. It was then pointed out that in his account to the group he had completely left out the fact that these parents must have beaten up their infant son.

In talking over this experience, it began to dawn on everybody in the room that the minister had been made to feel fear of the authorities, and failure. The couple had been unable to face such feelings and had succeeded in passing on their intolerable pain to the minister. He, being a kindly and receptive person, took it on board and was now actively taking their part in an uncritical manner. When he saw what happened as the discussion went on, he felt that he was regaining his self-respect and saw more clearly what his parishioners were struggling with in themselves.

What the parishioners did in this case with their feelings could be described as projection and when the minister started to have feelings which did not belong to him, we could say that he had identified with that projection. 'Projective identification' seems to work in this way; when faced with unbearable things about themselves, guilt at their own violence to their child, the parents split themselves and projected their bad selves into the nearest sympathetic person while remaining the good and outraged innocents. We found in the group that it is better to recognize these processes in some way than to be caught up in them. The pioneer of this mode of thinking was Mrs Melanie Klein,[2] whose work with disturbed children opened up a whole world of observation and understanding of children and adults which can be usefully applied to ministry.

In example 2 the ministers in the room did not speak as superior givers of insight but as fellow strugglers. They identified with their colleague because they had 'been there' and because they were not in the same impasse at that time, and felt free to point out some features in the situation to which he had been blinded. As a result, the minister heard what they had to say without feeling attacked.

The upshot was that the minister returned to the Social Work Office, negotiated a review meeting, and ensured that he was there to declare his continued interest in the family. He continued his pastoral care of the family, but this time in collaboration with the social workers. A case like this shows that the more upset and deprived parishioners are, the more important it is that carers help each other to get at the unrecognized processes. Small, but significant, shifts of perception and feeling can occur which allow ordinary work to be resumed.

As time went on, attendance at the group increased and when fifteen or more people were in the room the quality of contribution went down quite markedly. We decided to split into four groups corresponding to the Sector division of the hospital catchment area. People seemed to feel less anxious in the smaller group. Another factor in bringing down anxiety and increasing mutual trust was the reliability of the setting itself which could only be experienced gradually over time. Here we made a further interesting discovery:

There often seemed to be clear correspondences between some of the things that went on in the work group and some of the processes reported as occurring in the pastoral situations with parishioners.

Take the following features:

– the pastor has to know when to start and when to stop because the distressed person wants someone to cling to and at the same time is terrified of being a clinging baby for ever.

– the pastor needs to find and maintain a good distance with the person he is trying to help, not too close and not too distant. One reason for that is that we are dealing with the recurrence in adult people of mothering which was experienced as smothering on the one hand, or deserting on the other.

– the pastor needs to remain clear about his own task because the desperate person will try to bully or seduce him into all sorts of other activities because he wants the help of another human being, but fears that if he takes it he will be persecuted, belittled or swallowed up.

– the pastor needs to learn how to 'be there' for the person, if necessary for months or longer. Some of the worst experiences in adult life can occur in relationships which remind us of the parent who was physically present but not there emotionally – cut off, withdrawn and unavailable.

– finally, the pastor will have to know how to have his own feelings, think his own thoughts and make his own decisions during it all.

No wonder the great psychotherapist and thinker, Dr Wilfred

Bion, said 'You don't have to be super-intelligent to do this kind of work, but you do need to know how to use the intelligence you've got when you are under fire.'[3] When conditions of trust in a group develop, people experience the pleasure of being professionally listened to and responded to. All of these features can be detected in the following instance.

Example 3: A minister described how he had for some months now given many hours in ministering to a particularly tragic person who, after being chronicaly ill all his life with a rare disease, had now been told he was terminally ill with cancer. He had business worries and he lived with his parents who were deeply distressed about his condition. He sought help and support from his minister which at first was rewarding as he was a seriously religious person, widely read, intelligent and likeable. Now he was calling or phoning nearly every day and the minister was beginning to feel uneasy. The minister returned to the group a month later visibly shaken. He had, after exhaustive enquiries, discovered that there was hardly a shred of truth in the man's account of his situation. When confronted with incontrovertible evidence, the man denied having said these things and went on to gently chide the minister for believing ill of him. To his amazement, the minister began to feel guilty, for he was indeed secretly wanting to get rid of this tiresome person.

Everybody in the room had had similar experiences with 'impossible people', who were variously described by the psychiatrists as psychopaths and by the ministers as 'congenital liars'. Better is the description of such a person as a terrified infant who was ransacking the world for genuine care but when he couldn't get it, invented it by lying. When he *could* get it, as in the case of the minister's kindly attention, he became insatiably greedy, then became alarmed and anxious at his own unacceptable greed. He seemed to have the knack of pushing these unwanted feelings into the minister by projection. Without claiming that this must be the situation in precise detail, it had the merit of giving the minister a new perspective on an overwhelming situation. He reported later that he could deal with this man much better if he thought of him as being rather like one of his own toddling children when he was tired and naughty. What he held on to when the going was rough was the notion of pastoral work as the re-parenting of a lost child. He found himself on firm ground when he could reflect that it is uncomfortable to be a spoiled child who is not really over-indulged or 'loved too much' but rather is a child who was not loved at the beginning in a way that he needed and continues to be an unsatisfactory adult and generally to find other adults unsatisfactory.

A pastoral situation which had become impossible had, with the help of the group, been changed into one which was just plain difficult. The work of the group could be described at this point as making pastoral work the art of the possible.

Some members of the group began to feel the need of theoretical study and in increasing number have turned to the work of the Congregationalist minister and psychotherapist, Dr Harry Guntrip,[4] to find a working theory which does not de-humanize but does some justice to the depth and complexity of human beings in their relationships. Getting the drift of Guntrip's 'object relations' theory helps us to see the panicky child in the adult and to keep in touch with the adult and child both in ourselves and in the other.

Example 4: A young minister described, with some diffidence, the situation in which a woman older than himself had formed an attachment to him. He visited her during a prolonged illness and now she called him by telephone each day two or three times. He would try to keep her quiet by making the required home visit, but on arrival was several times disconcerted to find her attired in a brief kimono and offering him a seat on the sofa beside her. At these times he would cut short the visit and go. When he tried to refuse she began to threaten to kill herself.

The minister then broke off his account and told the group that he was feeling terrible. With guilt and distress he said, 'What on earth do you think of me. Please tell me what's wrong with me?' In the brief exchange that followed he went on to mention that his own mother had died recently after a long illness. He invited the group to discuss his family history. At this critical point in the whole course of the group project, an older minister took up the theme and spoke at some length. He said that over many years he had had this kind of situation to deal with and had come to the conclusion that these feelings were being delivered to the wrong address. He tended to treat the feelings with respect but kept referring them back to figures in the person's early past and first family and this helped him, the minister, to be less anxious about the sexual overtones which very easily sprung up and took you by surprise. The minister said that he had grown to thinking of people like this more as clinging children rather than as sexual adults. He saw his part as a minister becoming like an understanding father or mother to a small child who is longing for closeness. He added that he himself had gone off for some personal psychotherapy and found that that was very useful. He felt that there was a place for examining your personal hang-ups and blind spots but that the work group wasn't that place. The focus here had to be on the interactions with people who come to us, not on our own therapy.

One of the psychiatrists then came in and offered to work with the minister on this case. In the days to come he did just that and successfully worked with the woman, eventually admitting her during one of her disturbed phases. The minister continued to make use of the group as a means of distancing himself from the woman without giving up on her as her minister. He also went elsewhere to consider and resolve some of the personal issues of sadness and loss which had clearly been getting mixed up with his own work.

Looking back, I am convinced that the older minister was right although, at the time, it did seem to all of us that he was being ruthless and uncaring for a distressed colleague. In keeping to the task of the group he was keeping in touch with the competent adult in his younger colleague. To have taken up the personal difficulty and family history of the young minister would have been to yield to a kind of seduction and to risk patientifying and infantalizing him.

Example 5: A minister described his struggle to help a man for twenty-five years. He gave a detailed account of the man's unhappy childhood and youth when he had been bullied by a sadistic father. He had had two unsuccessful marriages, a number of children and a number of unsuccessful professional appointments. He had attempted to kill himself several times and always came back to the minister with endless requests for help, guidance, support and 'salvation'. The minister described himself now 'as being quite beaten in human terms but, of course, the Gospel might yet transform this man'.

He was asked if the man could do anything at all. To our

astonishment the reply came that he was extraordinarily gifted with those less able or younger than himself. He was in periodic demand among some young people especially in organizing successful concerts and summer camps but then when everybody went away he seemed to fade again and go off to live in seedy rooms and could be met endlessly walking the pavements.

It was put to the minister that he could tell the man just what he had told the group: that he, the minister, was 'beaten, humanly speaking, in his efforts to help him'. For twenty-five years he had 'witnessed to the inexhaustible riches of the Gospel and stuck at it with marvellous tenacity' but, said a colleague, 'Would it really be true that the Gospel would be less rich if he were to admit to the man that he was beaten and he needed the man's help? Had he not become identified with the Gospel rather than being a witness to it?' Or, to see it from the man's point of view, could we say that here was a frightened boy permanently needing to defend himself against his attacking Father by 'beating' Father?

The man's problem was that he had to beat the minister and bring his heroic efforts to nought, while the minister's problem was that he felt that he, as the bearer of the Gospel, had to win. The result was stalemate. As he unravelled some of these elements of aggression in the relationship which had rather dominated and preoccupied him the minister felt sufficiently free to move away to another job.

This case vividly illustrates one of the toughest problems in pastoral care and therapy. In disturbed people, interest, sympathy and concern arouses an unconscious counter-attack of sadism. If the minister becomes immersed in his guilt and his search for the 'right response', he fails to see the deeply conflictual nature of the patient's desires inside. The patient needs to make us feel, over and over again, that we are failing him, that we are unsatisfactory and are not giving him what he needs because that is what he experienced with his original parents and especially with his mother. At this point, we urgently need the help of colleagues to shift the centre of gravity from *our* guilt to *his* conflict. We, in the ministry, have a personal and professional weakness for clinging to the omnipotent fantasy that life can be wholly gratifying and conflict-free.

But, when it is working well, the group seems to take on the character of a tolerant and companionable parent who does not look down contemptuously at our efforts to be independent parents to these needy children that we have to take on. But rather the group, since it is composed of fellow strugglers in the ministry, offers a humorous perspective on work which shows us up in our weakness as well as in our strength. We are encouraged to maintain our hope.

Example 6: Sometimes the group had the effect of helping people to act more spontaneously as themselves. For example, a man asked his minister urgently to intervene. His friends had just been shocked and stunned by the behaviour of their teenage son. He had been caught stealing girl's underwear from a neighbour's clothesline. They were quite overwhelmed, unable to speak very coherently but were beginning to say that they would have to leave the town. The minister told the group that he was on his way after the meeting to see the parents with great foreboding. But, as he recounted the story, he told a story from his own childhood about his theft of a fishing rod, remarking that 'all kids steal something and he could remember the thrill of it to this day'. The group urged him to go and tell the parents the same story. He did and, in a slow and painful discussion, the parents began to face the fact that they had brought into the world a child who was sexual, curious and aggressive. They began to see that the lad's behaviour had more to do with his own frustrated curiosity about his sexual identity than with 'wickedness' or 'perversion'. They were eventually able to acknowledge something of their own marital conflict, take some responsibility for their own sexual lives, and to seek further professional help in marriage guidance. With that, the son's compulson to steal underclothes subsided.

In conclusion, one or two facts emerge quite clearly from our experience in the Mental Health Forums.

First, the need for personal help in these tough times is now growing at such a rate that if a psychiatrist, clergyman, or anyone else, has the necessary 'ear', capacity, and sense of commitment to people, to offer, he will quickly have his time and resources stretched to the utmost.

Secondly, if he or she is to continue for months and years rather than weeks giving help at a personal level to struggling people, he will have to give close attention to his own learning and development and abandon any notion of an 'arrived' state.

Pastoral care is the art of the possible; we are not going to work miracles.

Thirdly, the personal development and continuing learning that is the central issue if we are not going to raise human hopes and dash them again by our own panicky withdrawal is going to consist largely of the development of 'negative capability' described thus by John Keats in his letter to his brother:

> I had not a dispute but a disquisition with Dilke on various subjects; several things dovetailed in my mind, and at once it struck me what quality went to form a Man of Achievement especially in Literature and which Shakespeare possessed so enormously – I mean *Negative Capability, that is, when a man is capable of being in uncertainties, mysteries, doubts, without any irritable reaching after fact and reason.*[5]

Fourthly, our present day practice in the cure of souls needs a better, deeper and more comprehensive theory of the person in his inner world and social relationships than we have been using.

Lastly, psychoanalysis, like any other body of knowledge, can be used in a silly fashion to mystify others, but it can also be made to earn its bread. I suggest, as the result of these experiences with colleagues in the clinics and the churches, that, indeed, we can look in this direction for help to light up some dark places in our work and to develop a new language of the person in relationship which we can share with others.

9

Field Education and Ministerial Formation

David Lyall

Three models of field education

Recent developments within professional education generally
have seen an increasing emphasis upon experiential as well as
academic learning. In medicine, nursing and social work there
has been a growing awareness that disciplined reflection upon
practice must form a significant part of professional education.
In theological education, the expansion of the clinical pastoral
education movement over the past fifty years has had a profound influence upon the development of field education. While
the original emphasis of this movement was upon pastoral
education in clinical settings, its underlying philosophy and
teaching methods have been found to have a wider relevance for
learning about the practice of ministry. In particular, its
emphasis upon the practice of competent supervision has been
found to be of crucial importance in facilitating both personal
and professional growth in fledgling ministers, and some
consideration must be given to the nature of this supervision
process. First, however, it is necessary to examine another
important issue in field education, and that is the various ways in
which theory and theology may be related to the practice of
ministry. For an analysis of the relationship between theology
and practice in field education we turn to a paper by two
American Directors of Field Education.[1] J. D. and E. E. Whitehead
identify three models of field education, each of which represents a different understanding of the relationship between
theology and practice and a different perception of field

education's contribution to the overall goals of education for ministry. These models are: 1. field education as the application of theology in the practice of ministry; 2. field education as the development and acquisition of ministerial skills; and 3. field education as the locus of pastoral theology. The authors point out that, in practice, none of these three models exist in a pure form, most approaches to field education involving all three to some extent. It is helpful, however, to consider them separately.

1. *Field education as the application of theology in the practice of ministry.* Behind this model is the assumption that theology is learned in the classroom and library and then applied elsewhere. This understanding of theological education has deep historical roots. Schleiermacher[2] divided theology into three parts – Historical, Philosophical and Practical – describing the last as 'the crown of theological study'. Schleiermacher was the first major theologian to bring some order into the field of Practical Theology. His methodology, however, had unfortunate consequences, largely because of his premise that the relationship between philosophical theology and practical theology was in one direction only, the former fixing the subject matter with which the latter had to deal. More recently Barth, despite his well-known criticisms of Schleiermachers's general theological method, did not dispute this understanding of the nature of practical theology: 'practical theology is, as the name implies, theology in transition to the practical work of the community'.[3] When this theological method is carried over into field education, the clear implication is that no theological learning occurs in the placement. Practical learning there surely may be, but central theological assumptions remain unquestioned. The role of the supervisor is to help the student apply a predetermined theological position.

2. *Field education as the acquisition and development of ministerial skills.* In this model of field education there is a different relationship between theology and practice. Again the assumption is that theology is learned in the classroom, but whereas in the first model the focus is upon applying theology to the practice of ministry, here the concern is with the acquisition of skills.

Here the responsibility of field education is not the bridging of the gap between theological learning and religious practice but of putting the student in contact with areas of skill that fall outside the realm of the theological disciplines.[4]

The main danger of this approach is that the student will over-identify with the professional person from whom these skills are acquired. Thus if the principal aim of a placement is the development of counselling skills, the student may take on board the philosophy and methods of secular approaches to counselling to the detriment of a theological understanding of pastoral care. And what is particularly true of pastoral care placements may be more generally true of other areas of ministerial training. Thus an ordinand may gain experience in the techniques of the conduct of worship in isolation from a theological understanding of the nature of worship.

3. *Field education as the locus of pastoral theology.* In this model a conscious attempt is made to bring theology and practice into constructive dialogue, and to enable the learner to think theologically about the practice of ministry. The student brings to the placement a theological perspective which is still in the process of formation and there is also a concern for the acquisition of the skills of ministry. Now the task of the super-visor is to enable the student to ask questions arising from the experience of ministry in such a way that deepening theological understanding is of a personal nature and not a second-hand one derived simply from text-books and lectures. In this approach to field education 'the student learns how to allow his experience to question his theological tradition as well as how to allow the tradition to confront his life experience'.[5] Hopefully the student learns a method of theological enquiry which will provide a tool for continuing theological reflection upon ministerial practice enhancing his personal and professional identity as a minister.

At this point a caveat must be made. It is tempting to imagine that a good field education programme will have as its end-product a fully integrated theological student ready to begin a career in ministry. Such an animal does not exist! The integration of theological learning and ministerial practice is not so much a goal to be achieved as a process to be initiated, a process which will continue to be fed both by the acquisition of further experience of ministry and deepening theological insight. Here the purpose of field education, within the wider context of training for ministry is to help the minister-in-training learn how to learn, moving comfortably (or uncomfortably!) between the practice of ministry and theological reflection in such a way that each informs and enriches the other. Central to this process is a high quality of supervision and it is to an examination of this process that we now turn.

The centrality of supervision in field education

Supervision is a word with a variety of meanings and connotations, some of which are not very helpful in field education. The word has overtones of authoritarianism, of experts directing and 'overseeing' the work of subordinates. This is not the sense in which it is presently used. Here the emphasis is upon supervision as an educational process which has much in common with that found in other areas of professional education, particularly in areas such as social work and psychotherapy. But ministry is neither second-rate social work nor is it amateur psychotherapy, and the kind of supervision which is developed for theological education must be appropriate to the distinctive characteristics of pastoral ministry as opposed to other types of helping relationships.[6] This task has been carried out most extensively within the Clinical Pastoral Education movement as it has developed in North America over the past sixty years. More recently its underlying philosophy and educational methods have been found to have a wider application within theological education. The importance of supervision in ministerial formation is recognized by the following statement from an Anglican Theological College:

> The contribution of field training within the whole discipline of pastoral education may best be seen as the provision of that element which explores the context and the practice of Christian mission, challenges theological presuppositions and provides a valuable opportunity for the student to grow in the ability to express himself both as a Christian and as a minister. In accomplishing this task the importance of good supervision is paramount. The supervisor is one who enables the other person to grow in understanding and effectiveness as he engages in ministry.[7]

A more precise definition of pastoral supervision has been suggested by Pohly:

Pastoral supervision is a method of doing and reflecting upon ministry in which a supervisor (teacher) and one or more supervisees (learners) covenant together to reflect critically upon their ministry as a way of growing in self-awareness, professional competence, theological understanding and Christian commitment.[8]

Supervision is therefore an intentional activity, i.e. it is not a haphazard occurrence, and it is normally planned to take place during a pre-arranged meeting between supervisor and student(s). The focus of this meeting is educational and must be differentiated from other kinds of meeting with a different agenda. Thus a meeting for supervision is not:

1. *an administrative meeting.* While it is obviously necessary to set aside time to discuss such matters as the allocation of work, a meeting which deals mainly with administrative matters is not supervision in the sense in which that word is used in this paper;

2. *a tutorial.* It is not a tutorial because the learning in supervision depends upon students being enabled to reflect upon their own experience, not upon the supervisor's ability to teach from his;

3. *counselling.* In the course of supervision it may emerge that the student has personal problems with which he requires help. It is the generally accepted wisdom that in such a situation the supervisor should not at the same time assume the role of therapist, but that the student should be encouraged to seek help elsewhere. That said, it is often difficult in practice to separate supervision and counselling. For one thing it may be that the personal problem is directly related to an emerging issue in supervision, e.g. an unresolved bereavement may be inhibiting the student's own ministry to the bereaved. More fundamentally it is difficult for supervision to be truly pastoral if it does not model a concern for the student as a human being. Perhaps it is enough to re-iterate that supervision is not therapy and that the supervisor must guard against becoming so involved in a counselling role with the student that the primary educational objective is displaced.

The role of the supervisor

It is axiomatic that in supervision the role of the supervisor is crucial. The first fact to note about the supervisor is that almost invariably he or she is a practitioner, i.e. one who is exercising a professional ministerial role within a local congregation or other institution such as a hospital. This means that supervision is not the communication of theoretical knowledge by one who has not 'been there'. Normally the student will share in some of the on-going ministry of the supervisor. It follows therefore that an important dimension of the learning process (for good or ill) is the model of ministry portrayed by the supervisor.

As a corollary to the statement that the supervisor is normally a practitioner, it follows that the supervisor's primary professional commitment is not to the students but to the institution within which he works, i.e. to the congregation or hospital. His main task is that of parish minister or hospital chaplain and his work with students is entirely dependent upon the exercise of this primary role. The supervisor will therefore view with mixed feelings the advent of a fresh cohort of students. On the one hand, students provide interest and stimulation and there may even be a certain status in having students involved in one's work. On the other hand, supervision is time-consuming, each student bringing a peculiar configuration of problems. In addition to the time factor, the presence of students can be source of anxiety to the supervisor. That the students should be anxious as they begin to be involved with people at a deep level is understandable; that a supervisor should experience similar feelings is perhaps less obvious. Yet since the supervisor accepts responsibility for the students working with him, he may feel that any 'mistakes' made by the students will reflect upon him and damage his own standing within the congregation institution. The temptation therefore is to allocate to the students 'safe' tasks; but this strategem does not facilitate the students' learning. According to one of the pioneers of supervision in theological education:

> The anxiety is always first of all the supervisor's and his ability to use it is at the heart of supervisory adequacy. His ability to create programme structure and plans in which this anxiety can be used and not avoided is the dynamic dimension of supervision. If no student makes a mistake during a training period the odds are that the supervisor has so protected himself from anxiety by cautious assignment or overly close guidance that the student has not been learning much that he did not know already.[9]

Granted however that the supervisor has agreed to accept responsibility for a student, it is his responsibility to 'manage' the placement. Among the first tasks which supervisor and student will address together is the negotiation of a 'Learning Agreement', a concept embodied by the words 'covenant together' in Pohly's definition of supervision and which is fundamental to the practice of supervision.

The Learning Agreement

From the outset it is important that both student and supervisor be aware of mutual expectations. Indeed at the start of a placement there are various legitimate interests to be considered. There are the hopes and the needs of the student, the expectations of the supervisor, the demands of the placement setting and the curricular requirements of both the college which has requested the placement for the student and the denomination into which the student hopes to be ordained. The Learning Agreement is an attempt to clarify and embody these hopes, needs, expectations, demands and requirements.

The student will normally have some idea about what he wishes to gain from the placement. He may come to a congregation wishing to gain more experience in the leading of worship or of working with young people. It may well be that these hopes dovetail very nicely with certain tasks which need to be done within the congregation. Even so there are other factors to be considered. The college which has sent the student may have other ideas and feel that this student has already had enough experience in youth work and should spend some time visiting the elderly. Not only will the college have an idea about the kind of work which the student should be undertaking, it will also have the guidelines about the amount of time the student should be spending each week in the placement and a view about the kind of supervision which the student requires. These are the parameters within which the Learning Agreement must be negotiated. It will also include a reference to the arrangements agreed for supervision such as time and frequency of meeting and the method(s) which the student will use for reporting on work done, whether orally or in the form of written reports such as verbatim accounts of pastoral visits.

It may appear that the process described for negotiating the Learning Agreement is unnecessarily pedantic. However, time spent clarifying goals and expectations can lay the foundations of the kind of placement in which the student experiences maximum benefit.

One final point needs to be made. While all parties should make a conscious attempt to adhere to the Learning Agreement, it should not be regarded as totally irrevocable. There may be situations where something is to be gained by re-negotiation; the mid-point of a placement is frequently a time when initial expectations can be re-examined in the light of experience and new goals defined.

The process of supervision

So far the focus has been upon what might be called the 'externals' of supervision. While these are important they are, of course, subservient to the process of supervision itself, i.e. to what goes on between supervisor and student, for it is through the inner dynamic of this relationship that field education makes its contribution to ministerial formation. During the time set aside for supervision the student will come prepared to reflect upon some act of ministry in which he has been involved, e.g. the leadership of a Bible Study Group or a visit to a patient in hospital. The supervisor, in turn, will have a number of possible questions which he may wish to explore with the student. What actually happened (amplification of information given in the verbal or written report)? What did you (and others involved) feel about what was happening? How do you understand what was happening? How do you reflect theologically about this incident? (What theological issues were raised by the Bible Study? How does your theology of suffering relate to the fact of this man dying of cancer?) What alternatives were open to you? What are you going to do next (time)? What did you learn from this incident which is significant for your own understanding of ministry? These are some of the questions which the supervisor might wish to explore. He won't raise them all at once! Nor will he do so as though he were conducting a Gestapo-type inter-rogation. Supervision can only take place in the context of a relationship of developing openness and trust between supervisor and student. The student must be free to talk about his work without fear of condemnation, to think the unthinkable and to be affirmed in his own emerging identity as a minister. The temptation of the supervisor is to try and create other ministers in his own image. While the style of ministry modelled by the supervisor cannot but have an influence upon the student, the task of supervision is to facilitate the development of the student's own capacity to minister to others.

In a previous section of this paper three possible models of field education were described. It is now suggested that the approach to supervision outlined above is one which is congruent with the third model, i.e. Field Education as the Locus of Pastoral Theology. It is an approach which encourages dialogue between theological concepts and the practice of ministry allowing each to be informed by the other; it is an approach where the primary focus is neither upon the application of abstract theological concepts nor simply upon the acquisition of skills but upon the person of the student who is in the process of becoming a minister.

Other contributions to the supervisory process

While the relationship between supervisor and student is pivotal in field education, other resources may be helpfully involved in the supervision process:

1. *The peer group.* In some situations a supervisor may be working concurrently with a group of students, e.g. in a hospital chaplaincy setting. In such a case the group interaction is an important dynamic in the process of ministerial formation. Indeed the peer group experience is regarded as both normative and essential in the practice and literature of Clinical Pastoral Education. While individual supervision is still important, participation in a group of peers committed to the same task can, by virtue of the dynamics of a group which is both supportive and confronting, have a profound effect upon personal and professional growth. In a parish there is unlikely to be more than one student attached to that congregation, making the peer group experience impossible in that setting. It may however be possible for the theological college to provide a structure in which groups of students can reflect together upon the experience gained in parish attachments. It goes without saying that the leadership of such groups is a skilled task and that without such leadership harm can be done to students.

2. *Lay supervision.* In some congregations it has been found helpful to gather together a group of lay people who will contract to meet regularly with the student for the duration of the attachment. Many congregations have within them women and men who are professionally skilled in offering support to

trainees; there are others who are naturally gifted in this way. Such a group (quite apart from providing consumer response!) can be helpful in offering supportively critical feedback to students in a way not possible for the minister-supervisor.

3. *The support of supervisors.* From all that has been written above, it will be evident that supervision is not an easy task. It demands both skills and personal qualities on the part of those asked to supervise students. While colleges will be careful in their choice of supervisors and in their allocation of students to field education settings, much more needs to be done to enable supervisors to carry out their allotted tasks in the best possible way. In an ideal world these ministers would receive some basic training in the art of supervision. At the very least they require a forum in which they can explore with one another the problems encountered in their supervision of students, and it should be the responsibility of the colleges who seek placements for their students to provide this facility. Only by active co-operation between supervisors and the field education staff of the theological colleges can the resources of the church be channelled effectively into the making of its ministers.

Evaluation in field education

How may the contribution of field education to the making of ministers be assessed? If time and energy are being devoted to this part of theological education it may be assumed that those involved will want to know that this part of the enterprise is worthwhile. Further, if field education is truly regarded as an integral part of preparation for ministry then perhaps the educational outcome is as worthy of assessment as the more traditional aspects of theological education. Nevertheless it is much more difficult to assess in any objective way a field education placement than it is to mark an essay in one of the traditional disciplines.

There are at least three important questions to be considered:
1. What is the purpose of evaluation in field education?
2. Who might be able to contribute to the evaluation process?
3. How may evaluation be carried out?

1. *What is the purpose of evaluation?* Various parties have an interest in the evaluation of field education. The churches in which the students are accredited ministerial candidates will wish to know whether a student at the end of a course is ready to

assume the responsibilities of ministry. It may be sufficient for the appropriate committees that placements are 'sustained'. At a more sophisticated level, though, if these same committees are charged with arranging a further period of training for the candidate (e.g. as assistant minister or curate), then it is obviously helpful for the committee to have some idea of the candidates strengths and weaknesses so that these further placements can be of use both to the students and the church.

Colleges, too, have an interest in the assessment of field education particularly if the practical work of a placement is a required component of a course or degree requiring a grade or classification. It is notoriously difficult to give grades, let alone marks, for supervised experience. If pressed to do so, all a supervisor can do is to categorize a student as 'Excellent, 'Good', 'Average' or 'Don't-let-loose-on-any-account' and allocate a grade or a mark which the student might have been awarded for a comparable performance in a different kind of exercise. But this is inevitably very subjective and artificial. Therefore the tendency is either not to include the assessment of field education in making decisions about academic qualifications (other than to require a statement of 'satisfactory performance') or else to attach the assessment to some aspect of the placement which can be evaluated more objectively, e.g. to a report or project written up by the student. But both statements of 'satisfactory performance' from the supervisor and reports written by the student can skate around and never come to grips with an analysis of the real learning about ministry which did or did not take place.

The supervisor (and the congregational committee) will also want to ask questions at the end of the placement. Was the supervision offered helpful to the student? Were the agreed tasks ones which helped the student grow in understanding of ministry? Were they useful to the congregation (or hospital)? Do we want to have any more students?

And the student obviously has the biggest stake of all in the evaluation process. Will the placement be sustained? How will the supervisor's report affect the grade for the course or class of degree awarded?

But for everyone concerned there is a further, deeper question: to what extent does the process of evaluation contribute to the total educational value of the placement? Ideally the evaluation of field education should be part of the learning process, but for this to occur there must be a degree of trust and openness on the part of all concerned. There are in fact two possible rationales for the evaluation of field education. One regards evaluation as a basis of screening or forming judgments which may affect the career of the student; the other views evaluation as a vehicle of learning and growth which may also have implications for the future of the student, albeit in a more subtle and indirect way. Not only are these two approaches different, they may be a source of conflict, for if the evaluation is to be the basis of a judgment which will affect the student's future career, then the student may feel some inhibition about being open to the kind of exploration which is necessary for genuine learning. Unless the purpose of evaluation is clearly defined, the outcome will almost inevitably turn out to be an uneasy compromise between these two approaches.

2. *Who might contribute to the evaluation process?* All those involved in the placement will have a view regarding its success or otherwise. The student will be aware of the extent to which his initial expectations have been fulfilled, and as supervision proceeds will have a developing insight into his own strengths and weaknesses in ministry. The supervisor will also have opinions from a different perspective which may or may not coincide with those of the student. A lay group, representing a congregation, will have formed one or several opinions concerning the student's readiness for ministry. If a student has been part of a peer group fellow students will be able to provide significant feedback, both from hearing the student describe the various situations in which he has tried to exercise a ministry and from the experience of interacting with the student in the group. Can these various insights be fed into the process of evaluation?

3. *How may evaluation be carried out?* In the past the tendency has been for the student and supervisor to send to the college separate reports, neither report necessarily being seen by the other party. Since these were normally composed at the end of a placement, their impact was to a large extent extraneous to the total educational experience. A more sophisticated form of the above is to devise parallel questionnaires so that both student and supervisor address the same issues. If in addition both parties are required to read and sign the other's report, this has the effect of making the assessment much more integral to the learning experience. Neither party will necessarily agree with all

that the other has written, but the exploration of the differing perceptions will inevitably enhance the learning which takes place.

It is in those centres where field education has been most highly developed that evaluation has been taken most seriously. In many American seminaries students are required to spend an 'Intern Year' in a field education setting. This normally precedes the final academic year and a critical role is played by trained supervisors and a lay support group working in close collaboration with the seminary. In one divinity school, the basis of evaluation is an elaborate set of questionnaires completed by the student, the supervising minister, the lay committee, a consultant appointed by the School and (where applicable) the student's spouse. The raw data of evaluation is summarized in a computer print-out giving for the student information relating to different aspects of his or her ministerial practice. Of particular significance are the differences in perception expressed by the various parties involved in the placement. These perceived differences form a useful starting point for the further discussion which is central to the evaluation process. In the 1970s the (American) Association of Theological Schools undertook a massive 'Readiness for Ministry' project.[10]. In this study criteria of fitness to begin ministry were devised from the responses of five separate groups of people: 1. theologians and seminary professors, 2. lay people in parishes, 3. 'active' ministers, 4. denominational executives with responsibilities for the placement and supervision of ministers and 5. senior divinity students. Significantly, the dominant criteria were found to be in the area of the student's commitment and faith rather than in specific ministerial skills. Drawing upon this study, attempts have been made to devise instruments which might be useful in the evaluation of field education.[11] A weakness of this study is that it is based solely upon American data and further research is necessary to see whether the listed criteria of 'Readiness for Ministry' are relevant in other contexts. Its importance lies in the fact that an attempt is being made to bring some objectivity and reliability into a notoriously subjective process. Like field education itself, its evaluation is still at the beginning of its development.

Postscript

This paper has been based upon an understanding of field education which has become dominant in recent years, characterized by the identification of placements in parishes and institutions (mainly hospitals) as the main arenas of ministerial practice and by reflection upon that practice. There are various reasons why these settings have assumed such importance in field education, e.g. the existence of specifically ministerial tasks, mainly of a pastoral nature, which students might realistically undertake and of structures facilitating the development of appropriate supervision. Nevertheless, there is a growing edge to the discipline reflecting an awareness of other dimensions of the church's ministry, where the need to engage in social action is seen to be complementary to a ministry of pastoral care. New theological movements, e.g. Liberation Theology, point to a need for the church to minister within the structures of society. There is an accompanying awareness of the necessity to expand the horizons of field education through the involvement of students in 'social action' placements.[12] It is in response to these developments that field education will make a further contribution to the formation of the church's ministry in the world.

Notes

1. Divinity in Use and Practice

1. *The Table Talk of Martin Luther*, tr. William Hazlitt, Bell, London 1895, p. 179.
2. Luther, *Werke*, Wiemarer Ausgabe, TR1, No. 153.
3. The text of Mrs Thatcher's speech, together with a critical analysis, is to be found in Jonathan Raban, *God, Man and Mrs Thatcher*, Chatto and Windus 1989.
4. Roger Garaudy, *The Alternative Future*. Penguin 1976, p. 89.
5. Luther, W A, V. 84, 39f.
6. W. Pannenberg, *Theology and the Philosophy of Science*, Darton, Longman and Todd 1976, p. 435.
7. Ibid, pp. 438–39.

2. The Nature of Practical theology

1. Berlin 1850.
2. Ibid., pp. 27f.
3. J. J. Van Oosterzee, *Practical Theology, A Manual for Theological Students*, tr. M. J. Evans, London 1878.
4. Seward Hiltner, *Preface to Pastoral Theology*, Abingdon 1958, p. 48.
5. Oosterzee, p. 3.
6. Ibid., p. 2.
7. This observation is based solely on a study of works published in English until recently. There is now some revival of interest marked by the publication of the following: T. C. Oden, *Pastoral Theology: Essentials of Ministry*, (Harper & Row 1983) and Don S. Browning (editor) *Practical Theology: The Emerging Field in Theology, Church and World* (Harper & Row 1983).

8. Eduard Thurneysen, *A Theology of Pastoral Care*, John Knox Press 1962, p. 53.

9. Ibid., p. 15.

10. Seward Hiltner, *Preface to Pastoral Theology*, p. 20.

11. This is most clearly seen in an extended footnote (*Preface*, p. 222) in which Hiltner distinguishes his position from that of Tillich's method of correlation. Hiltner argues that Tillich is mistaken in supposing that the answers must always come from the side of theology. In his view a 'two way street' is possible:'... it becomes necessary to say that culture may find answers to questions raised by faith as well as to assert that faith has answers to questions raised by culture.'

12. Matt. 25.31.ff.; Luke 10.25–37; Luke 4.18.

13. It is significant that Hiltner's division of theological subjects has never been seriously discussed since he proposed it in 1958. Indeed even his close associates, contributing to a *festschrift* (*The New Shape of Pastoral Theology*, edited by W. B. Oglesby Jr.) make merely passing reference to it.

14. Thomas C. Oden, *Contemporary Theology and Psychotherapy* Westminster Press 1967 p. 57.

15. Dietrich Bonhoeffer, *Letters and Papers from Prison*, The Enlarged Edition, SCM Press 1971, p. 279.

16. We must dintinguish this question of *practical theology* from the questions more appropriate to *philosophical theology* of the relationship between 'Christian knowledge' and 'worldly knowledge' (faith and culture). The practical theological question is related specifically to action and interaction.

17. *The Church for Others*. Final Report of the Western European Working Group, Department on Studies in Evangelism, WCC, Geneva 1967, p. 15.

18. See especially Paul Lehmann, *Ethics in a Christian Context*, SCM Press 1963.

19. See J. C. Hoekendijk, *The Church Inside Out*, SCM Press 1964: H. Küng, *On Being a Christian*, Collins 1978; J. Moltmann, *The Church in the Power of the Spirit*, SCM Press 1977.

20. The conceptual models for the type of relationship proposed are to be found in Liam Hudson's converger/diverger categories (*vide Contrary Imaginations*, Methuen 1966 and *Frames of Mind*, Methuen 1968), in M. L. Johnson Abercrombie's description of the influence of schemata on the perception of new situations (*The Anatomy of Judgement*, Hutchison 1960) and in the distinctions between 'lineal' and 'non-lineal'

communication drawn by Marshall McLuhan and others (E. Carpenter and M. McLuhan, *Explorations in Communication*, Beacon Press, Boston 1960). There is now an increasing interest in the place of such imaginative associations in theology, see for example, S. McFague, *Metaphorical Theology*, SCM Press 1983.

21. Examples of such proposals can be found in church reports on nuclear war, legislation for abortion, changing attitudes to marriage, etc. The task of practical theology, however, is to subject the presuppositions and arguments of all such reports to critical scrutiny. Within the specific field of pastoral theology there is an interesting trend towards the sociopolitical dimension. See especially P. Selby, *Liberating God: Private Care and Public Struggle*, SPCK 1983. This, again, requires ongoing critical assessment from theological scholars as part of the general debate about the status of political theology.

3. The Bible and Christian Practice

1. Charles E. Curran, *Toward An American Catholic Moral Theology*, Notre Dame University Press 1987, p. 10.

2. Justin, *Apology* 1.61.

3. Literally, 'a calling to mind', 'recollection'.

4. Hippolytus, *Apostolic Tradition* 16–17.

5. The Cynic diatribe, as practised by Bion of Borysthenes, like the Stoic-Cynic diatribe in the hands of Zeno or Epictetus, was a lively communication: see the brief account in my *Kerygma and Didache*, CUP 1980, pp. 39–43. In the church, the address was often described as a homily (Justin *Apology* 1.67). After the fourth century *sermo* or 'sermon' was the more usual term. By this time, preaching was much more formal.

6. See the article by Chris Wigglesworth, 'Bible: Pastoral Use' in *A Dictionary of Pastoral Care* ed. A. V. Campbell, SPCK 1987, pp. 25f. and Stephen Pattison, *A Critique of Pastoral Care*, SCM Press 1988, pp. 106–133.

7. Karl Barth, *Dogmatics in Outline*, SCM Press 1949, p. 99.

8. Oliver O'Donovan, 'Paul Ramsey (1913–88)', *Studies in Christian Ethics* 1.1 (1988), pp. 88f.

9. Cf. E. D. Schneider (ed.), *Questions About The Beginning of Life*, Augsburg 1985, pp. 30–48.

4. Towards a Theology of Peace

1. Cf. Douglas J. Harris, *Shalom! The Biblical Concept of Peace*, Grand Rapids, Michigan 1970, pp. 13ff.

2. Ibid.

3. Cf. J. Pedersen, *Israel, its Life and Culture* I–II, London and Copenhagen, 1962, pp. 326f,; cf. more generally, pp. 311–335.

4. K. Stendahl in M. Black and H. H. Rowley (eds), *Peake's Commentary on the Bible*, Van Nostrand 1962, p. 775.

5. Cf. Steven Mackie, 'Gandhi, Martin Luther King, Catonsville and Greenham Common', *Modern Churchman* XXV, 4, 1983, pp. 3–9.

6. Cf. P. Freire, *Pedagogy of the Oppressed*, Penguin 1972.

7. Cf. M. L. King, *Strength to Love*, New York 1963.

8. E.g., his code of conduct for his followers, in *Why We Can't Wait*, New York 1964, pp. 63f.

9. He criticized but also learned from the 'Social Gospel' tradition of Rauschenbush, the 'personalism' of Brightman (to whom he was perhaps closest) and the political realism of Reinhold Niebuhr.

10. For a useful discussion of this, cf. John C. L. Gibson, *Genesis Vol. I* (Daily Study Bible), St Andrew Press 1981, pp. 77–80.

11. Cf. H. von Campenhausen, 'Christians and Military Service in the Early Church' in *Tradition and Life in the Church*, London 1968, pp. 160–70; A. von Harnack, *Militia Christi: The Christian religion and the military in the first three centuries*, Philadelphia 1981.

12. I have resisted the temptation to take 'unilateral' and 'multilateral' disarmament as the issues to be debated, since they represent the forms into which the political debate has bifurcated, and to adopt them here might have been to risk being programmed in one's thinking by the powers that be. Deterrence and de-escalation suggest themselves as practical policies which could be prompted, modified and guided by a discussion of theology and *praxis* such as we have attempted in this article. Otherwise, it is all too easy to adopt a theological rationale for positions held on other grounds. For example, if we cite on the one side the Anglican Report *The Church and the Bomb*, Hodder 1982 and on the other, *The Cross and the Bomb*, ed. Francis Bridger, Mowbrays 1983, the debate in England appears theologically barren: cf. also John Langan, 'Between Deterrence and Disarmament', *Modern Churchman* XXV, 1983, p. 17, and R. Gill, *The Cross Against the Bomb*, Epworth Press 1984.

13. Cf. John Eldridge, 'War, Peace and Power', in H. Davis (ed.), *Ethics and Defence*, Oxford, Basil Blackwell, 1986, pp. 188–

206, especially his discussion of Wright Mills' thesis that the power elite imposes its definitions of reality upon the people (pp. 190–192).

14. Tony Carty, 'The Origins of the Doctrine of Deterrence and the Legal Status of Nuclear Weapons' in H. Davis (ed.), op. cit., pp. 104–132.

15. Paul Ramsey used this kind of argument in *The Limits of Nuclear War: Thinking about the Do-able and the Undo-able*, Council on Religion and International Affairs, New York 1963. His closely argued thesis deserves to be taken seriously in relation to its context (viz. US policy after Cuba, as set out by the Secretary of Defense McNamara), and in terms of its purpose (viz. to encourage churches and individual Christians to consider the ethical implications of the deterrence policy actually adopted by the USA). What it lacks is a deeper theological dimension, such as that afforded by *shalom*. This would certainly reveal the limitations of the case Ramsey was arguing. Another attempt at the problem is found in C. Dunstan, 'Theological Method in the Deterrence Debate' in G. Goodwin (ed.), *Ethics and Nuclear Deterrence*, Croom Helm 1982, pp. 40–52. For a counter argument, see Roger Ruston OP, 'The Idols of Security', in A. Race (ed.), *Theology Against the Nuclear Horizon*, SCM Press 1988, pp. 155–168.

16. Mention should be made here of the US Catholic Bishops' Pastoral Letter, *The Challenge of Peace* CTS/SPCK 1983; cf. Henry D. de Knijff, 'The Churches' Growing "No" to Nuclear Weapons', *Modern Churchman* XXV, 4, 1983, pp. 42–47.

5. The Challenge of Church Decline

1. See Nigel Yates, 'Urban Church Attendance and the Use of Statistical Evidence, 1850–1900', in Derek Baker (ed.), *The Church in Town and Countryside: Studies in Church History*, Vol. 16, Blackwell 1979.

2. Sources: for 1851, see Horace Mann, *1851 Census of Great Britain: Report and Tables on Religious Worship England and Wales*, British Parliamentary Papers, Population 10, 1852–3; for 1887, see The British Weekly's *The Religious Census of London*, Hodder 1888; for 1903, see Richard Mudie-Smith (ed.), *The Religious Life London*, Hodder 1904; for 1928, see *The British Weekly*, 23 Feb., 8 March 1928; for 1962, see Leslie Paul, *The Deployment and Payment of the Clergy*, Church Information Office 1964; for 1975 and 1979, see Peter Brierley (ed.), *Prospects for the Eighties,*

Bible Society and MARC Europe 1980; for 1985, see *Church Statistics: Some Facts and Figures about the Church of England*, The Central Board of Finance of the Church of England, Church House 1987.

3. See Robin Gill, *Beyond Decline*, SCM Press 1988.

4. See Robin Gill, *Competing Convictions*, SCM Press 1989.

5. E.g. Michael P. Hornsby-Smith, *Roman Catholics in England*, CUP 1987.

6. Robert Currie, Alan Gilbert and Lee Horsley, *Churches and Churchgoers*, CUP 1977.

7. E.g. Bryan Wilson in *Religion in Secular Society*, Watts 1966 and *Contemporary Transformations of Religion*, OUP 1976: I review some of the recent literature on secularization further in *Competing Convictions*.

8. Stephen Yeo, *Religion and Voluntary Organisations in Crisis*, Croom Helm 1976.

9. OUP 1982.

10. OUP 1976.

11. Methuen 1987.

12. Heinemann 1955.

13. See further my *Competing Convictions*.

14. Leslie J. Francis, *Rural Anglicanism*, Collins 1985.

15. *Clergy Visitation Returns*, Auckland Castle Episcopal Records, held in the Department of Palaeography and Diplomatic, University of Durham: records after the formation of the Diocese of Newcastle in 1882 are held in the Northumberland Record Office, Gosforth, as are most of those for Dissenting Churches in Northumberland.

6. *Lex Orandi Lex Credendi*

1. José P. Miranda, *Marx and the Bible*, SCM Press 1977.

2. Michael Polanyi, *Personal Knowledge*, Routledge 1962, p. 199.

3. Those who wish to do so can turn to P. de Clerck, "*Lex orandi Lex Credendi*' Sens originel et avatars historiques d'un adage equivoque", *Questions liturgiques* et paroissiales, 59 (1978), pp. 193 to 212 and Geoffrey Wainwright, *Doxology*, Epworth Press 1980, pp. 218–283, esp. n. 523.

4. Karl Barth, 'The Gift of Freedom' in *The Humanity of God*, Collins 1961, p. 88.

5. See Maurice Wiles, *The Making of Christian Doctrine*, CUP 1967, chap. 4.

6. Brian Wicker, *First the Political Kingdom*, Sheed and Ward 1967, pp. 84–85.

7. Wainwright, op. cit., pp. 237–38.

8. Stephen Sykes, *The Identity of Christianity*, SPCK 1984, p. 277.

7. Theology and Ordained Ministry

1. Edward Schillebeeckx, *Ministry: A Case for Change* SCM Press 1981: see also Robin Gill, *Theology and Sociology*, Chapman 1987. Schillebeeckx's case is considerably expanded but not essentially changed in *The Church with a Human Face*, SCM Press 1985.

2. *Ministry*, p. 66.

3. Ibid., p. 39.

4. Ibid., p. 53.

5. Ibid., p. 56.

6. Bernard Cooke, *Ministry to Word and Sacraments,* Fortress Press, Philadelphia 1976.

7. Ibid., p. 21.

8. Schillebeeckx, *Ministry*, p. 75.

9. Ibid., p. 75.

10. Ibid. p. 76.

11. Ibid., p. 57.

12. Ibid., p. 155.

13. Cooke, op. cit. p. 161.

14. R. P. C. Hanson, *Christian Priesthood Examined*, Lutterworth 1979.

15. A. E. Harvey, *Priest or President?*, SPCK 1975.

16. Fenton Morley (ed.), *Partners in Ministry*, CIO 1967.

17. John Tiller, *A Strategy for the Church's Ministry*, ACCM 1983.

18. John Habgood, *Church and Nation in a Secular Age*, Darton, Longman & Todd 1983.

19. See Robin Gill in *Theology*, January 1983, and *Beyond Decline*, SCM Press 1988; see also Michael S. Northcott, *The Church and Secularisation*, Peter Lang 1989.

20. Bryan Wilson, *Religion in Sociological Perspective*, OUP 1982: see also Wilson in Philip Hammond (ed.), *The Sacred in a Secular Age*, California University Press 1984.

21. Wilson, *Religion in Sociological Perspective*, pp. 154–55.

22. Ibid., p. 156.

23. Peter L. Berger, *The Heretical Imperative*, Collins 1980.

24. Peter L. Berger, Brigitte Berger and Hansfried Kellner, *The Homeless Mind*, Penguin 1974.

25. Robert Towler and A. P. M. Coxon, *The Fate of the Anglican Clergy*, Macmillan 1979.

26. Anthony Russell, *The Clerical Profession*, SPCK 1980.

27. Ibid., p. 292.

28. See Mark Hodge, *Non-Stipendiary Ministry in the Church of England*, CIO 1983 and *Faith in the City*, CIO 1985.

29. Stephen Sykes, *The Identity of Christianity*, SPCK 1984.

8. The Group as Minister

1. See M. Leishman and B. Ritson, 'Working Together in Mental Health', *Contact*, no. 50, 1975.

2. See, e.g., Hannah Segal, *Klein*, Collins Fontana 1979; Elizabeth Bott Spillius, 'Some developments from the work of Melanie Klein', *International Journal of Psychoanalysis*, vol. 64, 1983.

3. W. R. Bion, *The Seven Servants*, Jason Aronson Inc., NY 1977.

4. E.g. Harry Guntrip, *Personality, Structure and Human Interaction*, Hogarth Press 1964; *Psychology for Ministers and Social Workers*, Allen & Unwin 1971; *Schizoid Phenomena: object relations and the self*, Hogarth Press 1968; *Your Mind and Your Health*, Allen and Unwin [2]1970.

5. John Keats, *Letters* ed., M. B. Forman, OUP [4]1952.

9. Field Education and Ministerial Formation

1. J. D. Whitehead and E. E. Whitehead, 'Educational Models in Field Education', *Field Education*, Vol. XI, No. 4, 1975, pp. 269–278.

2. F. Schleiermacher, *Brief Outline of the Study of Theology* (1811) John Knox Press, Richmond, Va. 1966, p. 125.

3. K. Barth, *Evangelical Theology: An Introduction*, Weidenfield & Nicolson 1963, p. 263.

4. Whitehead, p. 274.

5. Ibid., p. 277.

6. J. Foskett and D. Lyall, *Helping the Helpers: Supervision and Pastoral Care*, SPCK 1988.

7. I. D. Bunting, 'Field Education and the Goal of Supervision', *The Churchman*, Vol. 93, 1979, p. 321.

8. K. H. Pohly, *Pastoral Supervision*, Institute of Religion, Houston, Texas 1977, p. 64.

9. T. Klink, 'Supervision', *Education for Ministry* ed. Fielding, American Association of Theological Schools 1966, p. 183.

10. D. S. Schuller et. al., *Readiness for Ministry*, Vol. 1: Criteria, Association of Theological Schools in the United States and Canada 1975.

11. Van Dyck, 'Sharpening Goals and Evaluation in Field Education', *Theological Education*, Spring 1976, pp. 169–179.

12. J. L. Seymour, 'Placement Design: Defining the Context for Field Education', *Theological Field Education*, Vol. III, Association for Theological Field Education 1981, pp. 215–221.

Index of Names

Index of Biblical References